D1139393

Leeds Metropolitan University

17 0488077 7

YORKSHIRE AT WAR

YORKSHIRE POST

at heart publications

LEEDS METROPOLITAN
UNIVERSITY
LIBRARY

1704668077
M-5562l6
C9. 607
940.53081810222 YOR

DISCARDED

First published in 2006 by
At Heart Limited
32 Stamford Street,
Altrincham,
Cheshire,
WA14 1EY

in conjunction with
Yorkshire Post Newspapers Ltd
PO Box 168,
Wellington Street,
Leeds,
LS1 1RF

Image and text copyright: Yorkshire Post Newspapers Ltd

All rights reserved. No part of this book may be
reproduced in any form or by any means, including
information storage and retrieval systems without
permission in writing from the publisher, except by
a reviewer whom may quote passages in a review.

ISBN: 1-84547-109-1

CONTENTS

INTRODUCTION

Over the following pages, the photographs in this unique collection vividly tell the story of Yorkshire at war. The experiences of the North, East and West Ridings were very distinct, as were those across Great Britain as a whole, yet the war changed the lives of everyone, wherever their home was.

Yorkshire's war was the nation's war, in microcosm. Just as the East End of London's experience was different from that of Leicester, as Dover's was from that of Brighton and Canterbury's was different from Cheltenham's, so the experience of war differed from one part of Yorkshire to another. The populations of Hull and Sheffield and Middlesborough and the satellite communities surrounding them learned the full meaning of the "blitz", with well-known landmarks reduced to ruins over night, homes shattered, streets convulsed and the course of day-to-day life thrown into sudden and terrible turmoil. The air activity brought many shocking sights, but hardly any more extaordinary than that of a German fighter which made a crash landing in the very centre of Hull.

In the wool textile centres of the West Riding, fewer bombs landed – although those which did caused havoc enough – and the citizenry faced the daily grind of shortages and restrictions and, in the early days of the conflict, the daily dose of depressing news, with set-back piled on set-back.

Maintaining the people's morale in these key industrial area was absolutely vital, hence the significant role of ENSA with its travelling entertainments. In the countryside, it was all change as the formidable army of Land Girls took a hand in feeding the nation.

In these photographs can be glimpsed the indomitable spirit of Yorkshire – a spirit that imbued the whole nation.

Peter Charlton
Editor
Yorkshire Post

YORKSHIRE GREETS MR. CHURCHILL

Inspection of Troops

From Our Special Correspondent

IN THE WEST RIDING, Friday Night

THE Prime Minister, Mr. Winston Churchill, to-day toured a number of towns and villages in the West Riding, and wherever he went, though no previous notice had been given of his coming, crowds of people lined the streets and cheered. He visited troops at a number of places.

Put your clocks forward

Above: Prime Minister, Winston Churchill, on a tour of West Yorkshire during the War

PREPARING FOR WAR

Compared with the opening stages of the First World War when there was a sense across the nation of an exciting adventure ahead, and young men were impatient to "have a go at the Bosch", the mood, as captured in the photograph of volunteers who have assembled to sign up for military service in October 1939, is very different. Some are putting on a smile for the camera, but there is a dogged determination in the stance of many. There was work to be done, and they are ready to do it – whatever the cost.

A similar realism can be seen on the faces of the women collecting pots, pans, metal basins and other scrap for the war effort, while a certain belt-and-braces approach is evident in the picture of an instructor using a dustbin lid and long-handled shovel to demonstrate how to deal with an incendiary bomb.

Volunteers sign-up at Leeds recruiting office.

Below: Women collecting scrap metal for the war effort.

Bottom Right: An air raid shelter at Alwoodley in October 1939.

Bottom Left: Young Leeds men signing up for military service in October 1939.

NEXT IN DEMAND

Men of the 21-22 age group registering to-day in Leeds for military service.

Long-Awaited Move

Air raid shelters are now being built at some schools on the outskirts of Leeds ready for children to resume lessons. The picture shows the trench being made for the school at the junction of Nursery Lane and King Lane, Alwoodley.

Above: Yorkshire members of the L. D. V (Local Defence Volunteers) learn to use a rifle. Later this valuable organisation became the home guard. June 1940.

Right: A youngster is photographed at an air raid shelter at Bridlington beach, October 1939.

ALL QUIET ON THIS FRONT

An air raid shelter near the beach at Bridlington.

Below: An instructor at the Leeds A.R.P. School demonstrates how to safely deal with an incendiary bomb in 1941. He is seen pouring dry sand from a scoop on to the bomb while using a dustbin lid as a shield.

Bottom: Booby trap manuals.

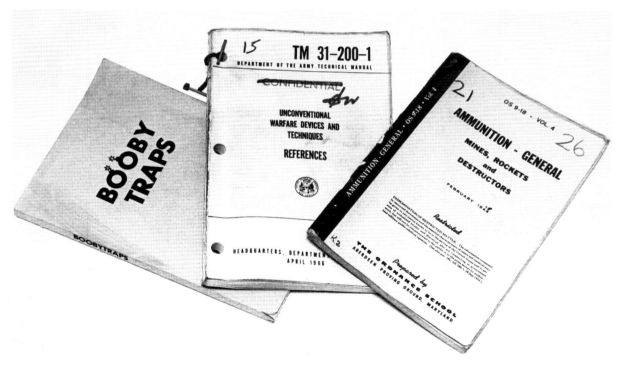

On the alert at an anti-aircraft post on a river bank during invasion exercises in the West Riding.

Above: An anti-aircraft post on a river bank during invasion exercises in the West Riding, January 1942.

Top: 'Warships Week' at Bull Green in February 1942.

Below: Lieutenant General Montgomery, Army Commander of the South Eastern Command, inspects troops of the King's Own Yorkshire Light Infantry.

Army Commander Inspects the K.O.Y.L.I.

A War Office photograph of Lieut.-General Montgomery, Army Commander of the South-Eastern Command, inspecting troops of the King's Own Yorkshire Light Infantry.

LEEDS METROPOLITAN UNIVERSITY LIBRARY

A FEW
CARELESS WORDS
MAY END IN THIS—

Many lives were lost in the last war through careless talk
Be on your guard ! Don't discuss movements of ships or troops

FOOD FACTS

Frugal but Festive

It will take more than Hitler to stop the British housewife from setting a festive table at Christmas time. Yes, the food will be the same—rations, vegetables, grain foods—no Christmas specials; because ship-saving matters more than ever now we have gone over to the offensive. But by dressing up the old favourites, by using little tricks of flavouring, garnishing and serving we can still put up a festive show. Stuffed flank of beef may take the place of turkey, and a little cold tea may be used to darken the complexion of Christmas cake or pudding, but we can still contrive a spread which will delight the children and warm the hearts of the grown-ups.

FOR FATHER — CHRISTMAS DAY PUDDING

Rub 3 oz. cooking fat into 6 tablespoonfuls of flour until like fine crumbs. Mix in 1½ breakfastcupfuls of stale breadcrumbs, 1 lb. prunes (soaked 24 hours, stoned, chopped) or any other dried fruit such as sultanas, 3 oz. sugar, 1 teaspoonful mixed spice, ¼ teaspoonful grated nutmeg. Then chop 1 large apple finely, grate 1 large raw carrot and 1 large raw potato; add to dry ingredients. Stir in 3 reconstituted dried eggs. Mix 1 teaspoonful of bicarbonate of soda in 1 tablespoonful of mixed lemon substitute and stir thoroughly into the pudding mixture. Put into one large or two small well-greased basins, cover with margarine papers and steam 2½ hours. This can be prepared overnight and eaten on Christmas Day.

WITH LOVE TO THE CHILDREN — CHRISTMAS FRUIT PIES

(A good alternative to mincemeat.)

Warm 1 tablespoonful of marmalade (or jam, but this is not so spicy) in small saucepan over tiny heat. Add ¼ lb. prunes (soaked 24 hours, stoned, chopped) or other dried fruit, 1 tablespoonful of sugar, 1 teacupful stale cake crumbs, or half cake, half breadcrumbs, ¼ teaspoonful mixed spice. Stir together until crumbs are quite moist. Remove from heat, add 1 large chopped apple; also some chopped nuts if possible. Use as a filling for small tarts or pies.

CHILDREN'S TREAT

1 Grated bar chocolate on freshly made biscuits gives the party touch.

2 Baked apples stuffed with war-time mincemeat are a splendid surprise.

3 Hot Cinnamon Toast for tea makes up for the shortage of cakes. Here is the way to make it.

Cinnamon Toast

Take 1 tablespoonful margarine, 1 dessertspoonful of sugar, 1 teaspoonful of cinnamon. Cream all the ingredients together, spread on hot toast and grill for two minutes.

THIS IS WEEK 22—THE SECOND WEEK OF RATION PERIOD No. 6 (Dec. 13th to Jan. 9th)

Tanks for Russia

Tanks being shipped for Russia at a British port.

The Navy's Minelayers

A picture taken aboard a minelayer of the Royal Navy, showing the men at their hard and dangerous work.

Opposite Page
Top: Mr W. W. Wakefield, M.P. Director of the Air Training Corps, presenting proficiency certificates to cadets of the Ilkley Squadron in April 1942.

Bottom Right: Men aboard a Royal Navy Minelayer demonstrate their work, April 1942.

Bottom Left: Tanks destined for Russia, July 1942.

This page: West Riding Squadron AAF pilots in their readiness hut at RAF Manston, March 1943.

Top: Men of the 68th (West Riding) Battalion on a training exercise at Owlerton Stadium, Sheffield, in May 1943.

Above Left: Final preparations for the Avro York transport plane, January 1944.

Above Right: Passing out of the 100th cadet glider pilot at West Riding Aerodrome, February 1944.

INDUSTRY

The roll of women underwent a dramatic and permanent change as British industry faced the demands of equipping the nation's armed forces to fight a world war. Women workers crowd the work benches of a bunting-draped Leeds factory on VE Day, and the woman on the factory floor of a Brighouse factory is not bringing round the tea trolley.

A reminder of the dangers of working in munitions factories is provided by the scene of industrious clog makers; the footwear they made would be worn by those who prepared the awesome 12,000lb Tall Boy and 22,000lb Grand Slam "earthquake" bombs, seen microcosm hanging in a Sheffield factory like carcasses moving through an abattoir.

They were carried by specially-adapted Lancaster heavy bombers and were put to devastating effect against V1 Flying Bomb launch sites and German submarine pens and other supposedly "indestructible" installations. Tall Boys were also used in sinking The Tirpitz.

Brighouse factory workers during the war

Top: Busy clog makers of Wakefield, August 1941. Clogs were in great demand from munitions workers.

Above Left: Dishforth Transport Section, 1944.

Above Right: More than a dozen trains loaded with tractors set off from the David Brown works in Meltham near Huddersfield.

Above: A power hammer beats out scythe blades for Russia in 1943. The hammer was built by the Beauchief Abbey Monks near Sheffield in the 15th Century. Here, steam has replaced water wheels as motive power.

Left: Railwaymen members of the Home Guard run to action stations on their light anti-aircraft gun at a railway depot as they prepare for daylight attacks by low-flying enemy raiders. April 1944.

Above: Men of the Resistance Corps sound a fanfare at the opening of a farmers' day during the Helmsley and District 'Salute the Soldier' week. May 1944.

Right: Sheffield-made cores for the 12,000lb Tall Boy and the 22,000lb Grand Slam.

Below: In tribute to the key role played by Sheffield's industry towards the war effort, the King and Queen leave their armoured vehicle to visit the works of Spear and Jackson Ltd, which was targeted by the Luftwaffe during the Blitz.

Bottom: VE Day at a Leeds factory.

As the headlines on April 30 from The Yorkshire Evening Post so graphically show, the daily dose of grim news in the dark days of 1941 needed to be countered. Hence the vital, morale-boosting role of the touring concerts staged by ENSA, progenitor of so many of the great post-war entertainers.

The pub sing-song played its part too, as did the irrepressible humour glimpsed in that market-stall sign: "Yes we have no bananas". The "Digging for victory" campaign had the more subtle effect of making non-combatants feel they could do something personal to help the war effort, even if it meant digging up the Stray at Harrogate to grow vegetables.

It was encouraging to know that every little helped.

A concert put on by the Entertainments National Service Association (ENSA) brings much-needed light relief during the war.

Below: Soldiers and locals lift their spirits during a singsong.

Bottom Left: War time rations.

Bottom Right: YMCA Tea car.

SNOOKER IN GASMASKS

Above: Snooker in gasmasks, April 1941.

To familiarise the wearing of gasmasks Morley police played a snooker handicap in them to-day. Their general opinion is that the innovation was amusing, and that it proved you can do most things with your gasmask on (writes a "Yorkshire Evening Post" reporter).

The colour of the balls is easy to distinguish, but sighting is another matter. Focussing the ball is the trouble.

The idea of this handicap in gasmasks was that of Councillor Alfred Horsfall, sectional commander of the Morley Special Constabulary. "As a game of snooker takes about half-anhour, it's a pleasant way of getting the players used to wearing the masks," he said.

Top: A pony-drawn sleigh is brought into use at Moortown, Leeds, during heavy snow fall, January 1941.

Bottom: Harrogate allotment holders busy at work on stray plots in Easter 1941.

Above: Mrs Ethel Newton and her seven-month old son, Gordon, are photographed in front of a barrage balloon in Albert Park, Middlesbrough, in August 1942.

Left: Youngsters dig for victory, Middlesbrough, 1944.

THE HOMEFRONT

Geography as well as strategic importance could determine the fate of a building, a street, a city, town or village during the German bombing offensive, hence the haphazard destruction visited up Bridlington. The docks and industries of Middlesborough and Hull were the real prizes sought by the Luftwaffe. On one such East Coast raid, an ME Bf109 escort fighter crash-landed in the centre of Hull, its wreckage guarded by three policemen. Sheffield suffered grievously, too, but Leeds received markedly little attention, considering its size and commercial importance. Its citizens were not required to endure the terrors of the blitz, and instead got on with supporting the war via worthy causes such as Wings for Victory.

Civilians might, from time-to-time, be shown some hardware, such as a convoy of tanks and other armoured vehicles careering over town-centre cobbles – and an impressive sight no doubt they were. Had the crowds been shown the Tigers and Panthers which made the Panzer divisions so formidable, however, they might have been less reassured.

One of several bomb-damaged streets in Bridlington.

THESE BOMBS
HAVE BEEN MADE HARMLESS
BY THE BOMB DISPOSAL SQUAD
HELP THEM

PARACHUTE
FLARE

LEEDS EVACUEES HOME FOR CHRISTMAS—MANY WILL STAY

Reunion scene at a Leeds station to-day when 1,500 secondary school evacuees came home for Christmas. It is estimated that at least half of them will not return to their billets.

There were many happy family reunions. Boys and girls arriving from Knaresborough were heavily burdened with haversacks, gasmasks, coats and attache cases.

The children on the whole looked well and happy. Most have put on weight during their four months away from home, and many who looked pale when they went away had the bloom of good health on their cheeks.

With the gradual reopening of Leeds schools it is clear that many parents have made up their minds not to send their children away again after Christmas.

On the other hand, Mr. L. Gaunt, Parkfield Road, Leeds, who was at the station to welcome his daughter Margaret, aged 15, said:

"She is settled in a good billet at Knaresborough. She is attending school regularly. We don't intend to interfere with the arrangements for her welfare.

"I am a believer in boarding schools, if parents can afford to send their children away from home. Margaret has never wor-

riod; she is quite happy. She lives with eight other girls."

But many other parents expressed an opposite point of view. Here are some replies to a "Yorkshire Evening Post" reporter's questions to parents on the subject:—

A Father.—The scheme has taught our boy to be more self-reliant. Now we want him back home. His school is being reopened.

A Mother.—I've had three children evacuated. Two are coming home to-day; the other returned early in the war. I'm glad to have them all back.

A Father.—We should have sent our boy back after Christmas but for a circular to parents on the reopening of secondary schools. That circular had had an unsettling effect.

Mrs. J. Blythe, mother of a boy of 16, said she did not know whether her son would go back to Knaresborough. For this reason, Carl, her son, is an art student. If the Art Master goes back to Knaresborough after Christmas, Carl will return; otherwise he will resume his tuition under the same master at Cockburn High School.

Above: Some of the bombs dropped in Sheffield during the Blitz.

Left: Evacuees return home to Leeds for Christmas in 1939.

Below: An incendiary device is tackled with a spade and dustbin-lid.

More Wounded Reach Leeds

"Evening Post" picture of the unloading at a Leeds hospital of ambulances bringing in wounded men from Normandy.

There were 131 stretcher cases and 5 walking cases in the latest batch arrivals. Many people wished to welcome them, but no civilians were allowed beyond the barriers on the central Station. A crowd waited on the streets outside the station and waved to the walking cases as they passed in buses on their way to hospital.

The wounded walking cases, including officers, gave cheerful smiles and waves. They included men from paratroop as well as infantry units. The hospital train was the third to arrive in Leeds within 36 hours.

A BRADFORD CONVOY

Among the convoy of wounded and sick which arrived in Bradford last night was Private Wendon Curtis, whose home is in Little Horton, and whose father is a member of the Bradford City Police. He is suffering from exhaustion.

Of the convoy 109, including 30 Germans, were taken to St. Luke's Municipal Hospital, 45 to Bradford Royal Infirmary, and 44 to Westwood Emergency Hospital. Those at Westwood include Gunner Frank Wroe, of Priory Road, Barnsley.

Members of the Bradford Services for the Wounded distributed cigarettes, and collected the postcards on which the men had scribbled messages to relatives. To-day members of the Service visited the men with handkerchiefs, tooth brushes and other toilet requisites. Safety razors are badly needed. Gifts of such razors should be handed in at the Services headquarters, 21, Market Street.

Above: A Middlesbrough motor barge 'sweep', sunk by gunfire on The Tees, had 164 bullet holes in her hull.

Left: Casualties from Normandy are brought to Leeds, June 1944.

Below: Bomb damage in Wakefield.

Above: A 'War Weapons Week' parade in Bull Green in December, 1940

Below: Troops in
Horton Street, 1940.

Left: VE Day celebrations in Southgate, June 1945.

Below: 'Salute the Solider Week' on parade in 1942.

HULL

Above: Hull's local residents do their
best to clear the debris caused by
German bomb attacks.

After a German Air Raid on Hull

A *"Yorkshire Post"* picture just released for publication of a Hull store in the centre of the city, wrecked in a recent German air raid.

Above: The Yorkshire Post reports on a heroic act following an air raid in June 1941.

Left: A local boat on the water in 1940.

Below: Some of the children of Hedon School, near Hull, who sacrificed part of their Christmas holidays to assist in sorting, packing and moving ten tons of emergency food reserves in January 1942. They were later thanked by the Minister of Food, Lord Woolton.

Police in Masks

Seen in Leeds To-day

Leeds police are to wear their gas-masks for a quarter of an hour every other day while on duty. This order by the Chief Constable (Mr. F. Swaby) is for the double object of getting the police used to their masks and of setting a good example to the public.

Leeds people are still very slack even in the matter of carrying their masks, let alone that of wearing them; this despite the Government's desire that everybody should have the mask handy at all times and should wear it periodically to get accustomed to it.

Air raid wardens and members of the A.F.S. have also been asked to wear their masks at intervals.

Keighley police started to-day to wear their gasmasks on duty. They will wear the mask for a certain period each day.

Above: Bomb damage in Queen Victoria Square.

Left: Gas masks were issued to everyone, including the police. April 1941

Right: Ark Royal Week, February 1942

Above: Lord Mayor, Miss J. B. Kitson and J. Milner MP show the total amount raised during the Leeds Wings for Victory Week in 1943. Also in the picture is Sir Charles Davis, chairman of the Leeds Savings Committee.

Left: Leeds War Emergency Committee.
Back row, from left to right:
Ald. J. Rafferty,
A. T. Wilson,
D. A. Radley,
Ald. H. W. Sellers.
Front row, left to right:
Ald. James Croysdale,
Ald. C. V. Walker,
Sir W. Bartholomew,
Ald. G. Brett.

THE GLORY ON THEIR WINGS...

WINGS FOR VICTORY

Top the 5,000,000 Target!

TONG ROAD DEPOT
R. D. P.

Below: The Youth Week Grand Final,
Roundhay Park, September 1942.

Bottom: The Tong Road Depot
1943 Infantry.

Yorkshire at War

Opposite Page
Top: Leeds messenger corps
in 1944.

Below: Trophies won by 1418
(South Leeds) Squadron ATC
between 1943 and 1944.

Some of the wounded men photographed on arrival in Leeds yesterday.

Wounded from India & Burma Arrive in Leeds

Top: Six airborne men from
Yorkshire who came out of Arnhem.
Pictured from left to right are
W. Clark (Leeds), Private H. Blakeley
(York), Private C. Pryke (Ossett),
Private H. Spinks (Leeds),
Private C. Stones (Leeds) and
Private E. Westerman (Leeds).
October 1944.

Left: Marching past the
Town Hall in June 1945.

Right: The Yorkshire Post
reports on wounded arrivals from
India and Burma in January 1944.

Above: Midnight victory celebrations at Leeds Town Hall on 15th August 1945.

Right: The NAAFI club, Albion Street, on VE Day.

Opposite: Albion Street decorated to celebrate the end of the War.

WE HEARTILY
THANK THOSE
WHO CAME
TO OUR ASSISTANCE
A.E.LEE & FAMILY

Above: The aftermath of Sheffield's blitz

Right: Locals sort through the rubble after bomb attacks.

12th December 1940.

Below Left: The Blitz in High Street showing the top of Angel Street.

Below Right: A Wicker tram lies overturned following air raids in Sheffield.

Above: Marple's Hotel
lies in ruins.

Left: The King and Queen and
the Lord Mayor of Sheffield visit
bombed dwellings after the
Sheffield blitz.

Above: Angel Street
during the Blitz.

Opposite: A fleet of
Telegraph and Star delivery
vehicles, including horse and
traps, motorcycles and a variety
of trucks, lines up ready to bring
Sheffield locals all the news that
was allowed to be circulated in
those dark days of war.

Below: An army convoy is photographed outside York Minster in 1943.

Above: US soldiers from New York, Alabama, Kentucky and Tennessee are pictured on a tour of York with guide Mr H. Tudor, Northern PR officer of the British Council, in 1943.

Opposite: A busy day at the farm of Mrs M. Milner, near Askham, in March 1944.

The Second World War saw the first mobilisation of the civil population in this country's history. Joseph Goebbels promised "Total War" in his famous speech of 1943, but in Britain there was already a very clear understanding of what "total" war meant, and women knew especially well. They were expected to be as much a part of the nation's war effort as any front-line soldier; in Sheffield they set a nationwide precedent by taking over the deployment of barrage balloons. More famously, thousands of Land Girls helped maintain the production of food, and as can be seen in one photograph after another, they abandoned the niceties of fashion for the hard-wearing, shapeless, practical clothing which farming demands, and they wore it with pride.

The war, of course, impinged on women's lives in other ways; they had to learn how to feed their families on the meager provisions allowed by rationing, and the advertisement for Sanizal disinfectant – "emergency sanitation for air raids," is testament to an unspoken condition with which many mothers and housewives no doubt became familiar.

Above: Early on in the war,
it was decided that women
would play a vital role.
Here WAAF's are learning
how to inflate a balloon at the
Sheffield repair depot.
The city balloon defences
were the first in the country
to be handed over to women.

Right: A Yorkshire gun site,
operated by chief controller
Mrs Jean Knox.

Above: Joan Sugden (extreme right) is photographed with fellow Wrens during the war.

Left: Yorkshire land girls marching from a church service at Little Poulton Hostel near Grantham.

Below: Mrs Winnie Wightman of Armley, a member of the Women's Land Army, feeds the poultry on Mr. J. W. White's 'Elms Farm' near Pickering, where she is training. August 1939.

Above: The Women's Land Army in training at the Durham County School of Agriculture at Houghall in September 1939.

Left: The Land Army girls at the opening of their Ripon hostel in 1941.

Above: Women's Junior Air Corps march past the Civic Building in Rothwell in 1942.

Left: Girls from the Women's Land Army Hostel, Easingwold, December 1941.

Above: Ark Royal Week Parade, 1942.

Left: Sally, Marie and Edith, the only gang of women platelayers in the North of England, at work on the LNER near Sheffield in 1942.

Below: The Women's Land Army, December 1942.

Bottom: Girls feeding ten-week old chickens at a poultry farm in March 1943.

Above: ATS girls training at a
Northern Command Emergency
Cooking Centre in 1943.

Opposite: Two women assist a
local farmer in Appleton Roebuck,
July 1943.

MINISTRY OF FOOD

REGISTER NOW

FOR

MEAT

YOU must register now to enable the Ministry of Food to

distribute meat fairly to the shops throughout the country,

and to assure YOU of your fair share when rationing begins.

WHAT YOU HAVE TO DO NOW :—

1 Put your name and address on the counterfoil at the bottom of the Meat Page of your Ration Book NOW.

2 Write on the inside front cover of your Ration Book the name and address of your butcher.

3 Take your Ration Book to your butcher and let him write his name and address on the meat counterfoil and cut it out.

4. If you move to another district, take your Ration Book to the local Food Office in your new district.

5 The numbered coupons *must not* be cut out yet. This will be done by your butcher when you do your shopping after meat rationing begins.

6 If you have registered for meat before Christmas, this registration was unauthorised. You may let it stand, and it will then be effective. Or, if you wish, you may register now with another butcher by recovering the counterfoil from the butcher who holds it and taking it to the butcher you now choose.

YOU ARE FREE TO CHOOSE ANY BUTCHER YOU LIKE

YOU MUST REGISTER NOT LATER THAN

MONDAY 8TH JANUARY

AN ANNOUNCEMENT BY THE MINISTRY OF FOOD, GT. WESTMINSTER HOUSE, LONDON, S.W.1

AIR RAIDS

SANIZAL DISINFECTANT

FOR

EMERGENCY

SANITATION

Be prepared —

buy two bottles to-day

whilst you can still do so !

Newton, Chambers & Co. Ltd., Thorncliffe, nr. Sheffield

Above: The Women's Junior Air Corps march past the Civic Buildings, Rothwell, for the visit of the Princess Royal during the war.

Above: Women were active in the National Fire Service during the war. This squad of first year firewomen from the Middlesbrough unit were on a general training course at a residential training school in County Durham during the spring of 1943.

Left: Monica Bradley (far right) and wartime colleagues find time to relax in Brussels.

VINES
Fashion Stylists
...COIGNE ST.,
Boar Lane,
LEEDS.
Tel. 22122.

SEDDON 6-TON
Official Distributo
FRANK H. I
39-41, CAMP ROAD,
Reasonable delivery on receipt
Operators Interested in 8

The Yorkshire Post
and Leeds Mercury

LEEDS, FRIDAY, AUGUST 4, 1944

LETING EDS

"v Cases," ector

7, traders will be given edits. They have also d to draw on reserve

ngements have also respect of unrationed

...ease-Lend cooked tripe r reception areas. The d be increased if the p. Supplies of manu- s to all manufacturers, and general butchers, d by 50 per cent. since it increase, one of 25 a made on July 9 been instructed to of temporary ration far as stocks permit. livestock officers have take local action to

s of tomatoes to dis- sociations are being ly in step with the uces. Imported fruit l be similarly adjusted he occasion arises. The have assisted the trade lties in transporting s have arisen. to bakers of fat, sugar. c., are being increased num of 10 per cent. of ight weekly allocation. upplies have been made me areas

all concerned in the r 2,100 official evacuees was expressed at last g of the Dewsbury Town e Mayor (Alderman T. ury people generally, he onded exceedingly well accommodation. added: "We have had a customers and, although are smiling just now at have, as they imagine, he billeting officers. ll come when the next ees arrives."

HEAVY HOLIDAY BOOKINGS

BUS QUEUES IN LEEDS

"We have no idea whether the holiday traffic will exceed that of last year, but bookings are already very heavy to all parts," an official at Leeds City Station told "The Yorkshire Post" yesterday.

Bookings have also been fairly heavy at Leeds Central Station. "They are for both coast and country," said an official.

"The traffic is definitely heavier than last year, but it is difficult to pick out any one centre where pressure is more pronounced than the rest," said a representative of the West Yorkshire Road Car Co., Ltd., at the Vicar Lane bus station.

"There have been queues all the week, but all have been getting away. It is clearly holiday-at-home traffic," he added.

Lakeland

In Lakeland, most available hotels and boarding-houses were booked for August several months ago, and visitors arriving this week-end without having previously booked rooms will have a hard task in finding accommodation. Next week Kendal will stage a holidays-at-home programme on an elaborate scale.

Whitby

There has been a steady flow of visitors to Whitby during the week, and the limited accommodation is being severely taxed. The beach lift is now available to visitors, and bathing is in full swing.

Holidays-at-Home

Wakefield's Many Attractions

From Our Own Correspondent

Wakefield, Thursday

Wakefield's Holidays-at-Home pro- gramme has had a setback with the postponement of its agricultural show on account of foot-and-mouth disease. Councillor Harry Watson, honorary organiser of the programme, announces that the show will prob-

Goole Schoolgirls Help with the Flax Harvest

Two girl pupils of Goole Grammar School, helping to gather the flax harvest in the Selby district.

Suspension of Leeds Parcels Service: Traders' Protests

Leeds Transport Committee's decision, confirmed by the City Council this week, to close the Cor- poration Parcels Department, except for the delivery of hot meals to schools, is a serious blow to some tradesmen.

Several have sent letters to "The

Co., 99, Mabgate, Leeds, whose letter you published recently, or to get in touch with their society if members of the Chamber of Trade."

Mr. W. Vane Morland, General Manager and Chief Engineer of the Transport Department, told a "Yorkshire Post" reporter yesterday that the Transport Committee had

NEW HULL P.A.C. SCALES

City Council Gives Its Approval

From Our Own Correspondent

HULL, Thursday

What the Lord Mayor (Alderman

News of

W.A.A.F. KILLED

Miss Gwendoline Joan Dannatt (21), daughter of Mr. and Mrs L. Dannatt, Haig Avenue, Scunthorpe, has been killed in London by enemy action. She had served with the W.A.A.F. for three years.

Servicemen's Leave Centre

Commander R. H. Torbock, R.N. and Mr. H. C. Torbock, R.A. sons of the late Mrs. Joseph Torbock, Crossrigg Hall, Cliburn, near Penrith, are lending Crossrigg Hall as a leave centre for Dominion and Colonial Servicemen, as a gesture of appreciation for the hospitality they have been accorded in many parts of the world.

Pianoforte Recital

A lunch hour pianoforte recital was given at the Mechanics' Institute, Bradford, yesterday, by Erik Brewerton.

Knaresborough's Salute

The final figure for Knaresborough Salute the Soldier Week is £334,694, an average of £42 9s. 6d. per head. Small savings amounted to £116,294 or £14 15s. 2d. per head. Knaresborough has the best return in Yorkshire.

Northern Casualties

Captain T. Dawson Whaley (34), elder son of the late Mr. and Mrs. James Whaley, of Rookhurst, Hawes, has been killed. Before the war he was an assistant solicitor in Newport, Mon

Other casualties include :—

Missing

Flight Sergeant Peter Cameron, whose mother formerly lived in Leeds. Sapper Fred Croad (31), Scout View, Hall Bank Lane, Mytholmroyd. Fusilier J. H. Crouch (22), Temple View, Bargate, Richmond.

Prisoners of War

Private Arthur Law, Coleman Road, Holbeck, Leeds. Private George Major (19), Barrowcliff Road, Scarborough.

Wounded

Sapper Walter Simpson (29), Gainsborough Street, Hanover, Leeds. Sapper Harold Ambler (24), Old Green Yard, South Kirkby. Trooper Gerald Walter Neale (22), Post Office, Cudworth. Serjeant Alan Greenwood (26), Fern Avenue, Ashby, Scunthorpe.

Believed Killed

Private Arnold Palmer (26), Mayes Street,

Above: Women's Land Army girls at
a ploughing competition in Tadcaster
in February 1945.
Pictured from left to right are:
M. Gallaghan (Leeds),
Dorothy Grange (Bradford),
Doris Brunt (Barnsley)
and Muriel Topper (Bradford).

The newspaper headlines trace the war's course, from the darkest days –
"War situation worsens" – through moments of when there was something to celebrate –
"Bismarck sunk" – until victory begins to look a real possibility –
"German's pursued across Tiber" and later "Invasion of Northern France goes to plan."
until "Allies now fighting five miles inside Germany."

Pictures of the fighting men perhaps disguise the reality of their experiences. Men of the
6th battalion York and Lancaster are seen resting during the Italian campaign, but not seen
is the hard, relentless slog with little sleep and no creature comforts besides, perhaps a
bank to lean against while aching feet get a brief respite. And there is the "Smile please"
photo of the nine Yorkhiremen rescued after nine days adrift at sea without food or water.

Men of the 1st Battalion York and
Lancaster Regiment passing through
Belpasso, Sicily, in 1943.

Registered for transmission in the United Kingdom
PRICE THREE HALFPENCE

TAX FREE KNITTING WOOLS
All Kinds & Colours
Stephenson's
KING EDWARD St. LEEDS
Tel. 27608

Yorkshire Evening Post
LEEDS SATURDAY, APRIL 5, 1941 No. 15,748

LATEST
Good Whisky—
JOHNNIE WALKER
BORN 1820—STILL GOING STRONG

JUGOSLAVIA ISOLATED: FRONTIERS NOW CLOSED

WAR SITUATION WORSENS

Intensified Nazi Warnings

It was "hardly possible" for the situation which has to-day developed between Jugoslavia and Germany to become worse, said a Nazi Foreign Office spokesman this afternoon.

A Royal decree issued in Belgrade to-day ordered the armed forces of Jugoslavia into a state of preparedness for war.

The German, Italian, Hungarian, Rumanian and Bulgarian frontiers with Jugoslavia were all reported by Belgrade Legations to-day to have been permanently closed, said an Associated Press message from Belgrade. A Budapest report was that all traffic on the Danube within Jugoslav territory is stopped.

Berlin has to-day resumed and intensified its propaganda attacks on, and warnings to, Jugoslavia.

DIPLOMATIC STAGE ENDED

A Nazi Foreign Office spokesman said this afternoon that diplomatic intercourse between Germany and Jugoslavia had practically ceased and added that it was "hardly possible" for the situation to become worse.

Squadrons of Jugoslav fighter 'planes flew over Belgrade in a northerly direction shortly after noon.

One neutral diplomat said that through his ontacts with the Simovitch Government he could state definitely that the "diplomatic stage had ended," and that it was now just a question of hours "before a new stage began."
—Associated Press.

The British United Press reports Berlin officials as saying to-day that there was practically no diplomatic contact between Berlin and Belgrade, and that the situation could hardly be worse.

JUGOSLAV MOVES

Fears of Week-end Attacks

Belgrade, Saturday.

Fears that Hitler may attack Jugoslavia this week-end are being expressed in diplomatic quarters in Athens. New preparations for war were being made in Jugoslavia while the Jugoslav Cabinet assembled for an important meeting in Belgrade last night.

Jugoslav anti-aircraft batteries and fighters at the same time brought down a foreign aeroplane which flew over Ruma, north of Belgrade.

Berlin, while returning to its hymn of hate against the Jugoslavs, categorically denied reports that relations with Jugoslavia had been severed.

In Zagreb, chief city of Crotia, all private cars were requisitioned by the military authorities.

The Jugoslav youth movement, Sokol, called on all its members to be ready to fight in defence of Jugoslavia by Monday, according to a Belgrade Radio announcement picked up in Budapest. The organisation also appealed for new members and advised its women to register for Red Cross and other duties.

The Frontier Plans

The Budapest "Kis Ujsag," published reports that the frontier with Jugoslavia had been closed by the Jugoslavs, who were mining bridges and roads. No confirmation of this report has yet been received. Heavy Jugoslav motorised units, the paper claimed, were being concentrated on the Hungarian frontier to the south of Pecs, while Jugoslav sappers were being held in readiness.

Britain, Greece, Jugoslavia and Turkey, according to the most reliable reports available in Athens, are continuously in touch with one another and are preparing for join action in the event of an Axis attack on Jugoslavia. To-day, the Turkish Assembly is expected to raise the age limit at which reservists can be mobilised from 45 to 60.—British United Press.

"ANY HOUR NOW"

Cabinet Sitting Early This Morning

Following a 4½ hour session of the Jugoslav Cabinet which ended at 2.30 this morning, observers in Belgrade saw in the refusal of solemn-faced ministers to discuss the meeting, grounds for the fear that war might come "at any hour now."

No communique was issued, but according to a semi-official explanation, the "critical foreign question" was discussed. Only a few ministers went home to bed after the meeting. Most returned to their offices.

The Cabinet meeting was the latest of many developments in the tense Balkans and followed the disclosure that King Peter had ordered the mobilisation of the entire "military might of Jugoslavia" in a proclamation issued on Tuesday.

Ankara reported that Turkey was steadily increasing her defences. There were persistent rumours in the Ottoman capital of a new form of Balkan front against Axis aggression. An official Jugoslav source in Ankara said that it might take the form of a mutual defensive alliance between Greece, Jugoslavia and Turkey with British backing. The Anglo-Turkish staff talks now under way in Ankara will probably last for a fortnight.—Associated Press.

FRESH MEASURES

Jugoslavia, faced with reports of menacing German troop movements on the one hand and "peace" hints from Berlin and Rome on the other, is taking fresh measures for her safety.

Budapest reports state that a "Jugoslav armoured division" is concentrated in the Daranya region. As Nazi troops are reported to be passing through Budapest towards the Jugoslav frontier, Hungary also is taking precautions. All doctors and chemists have been ordered to register their names and addresses with the authorities by April 15 and the population of Budapest have been requested to make A.R.P. preparations.

Nazis Threaten Hungary

The Hungarian Cabinet met yesterday after Bardossy, the new Prime Minister, had received the German Minister in Budapest, Erdmannsdorff. The Nazis are said to have demanded active Hungarian military aid against the Jugoslavs and to have offered Hungary, as a bribe, the Banat areas of Jugoslavia. At the same time, Hungary was threatened with dismemberment if she refused.—Press Association.

Cruisers Bombed at Brest

SHIPS STRADDLED BY BIG BOMBS

An Air Ministry communique issued this afternoon says:—

Last night a strong force of aircraft of the Bomber Command continued the attack on the naval base at Brest and on the battle cruisers Scharnhorst and Gneisenau. The ships could be clearly identified in the moonlight, and the attack was pressed home with great resolution. Some of our aircraft bombed from very low levels; and good results are reported. Sticks of heavy bombs were seen to straddle both ships.

Near one of them a large fire broke out, and several fires were started among stores of oil and warehouses.

Other aircraft attacked oil stores at Rotterdam and industrial targets in the Ruhr. One of our aircraft is missing.

Yesterday, during daylight, aircraft of the Bomber Command attacked two naval auxiliaries off the west coast of France. One was hit and left sinking. Machine-gun attacks were also made on a number of minesweepers. One aircraft is missing from these operations.

It is now confirmed that an aircraft of the Bomber Command destroyed an enemy fighter while flying to the attack on Brest on Thursday night.

Third Raid This Week

It was the second night in succession, and third time this week, that the German occupied naval base at Brest had been bombed.

British aeroplanes were over Western Germany last night, said the official German news agency in Berlin to-day. A few bombs were dropped, but no damage was caused, said the agency. —British United Press.

GERMAN KULTUR!

Leeds "Books and Freedom" Exhibition

When war broke out Leeds Art Gallery pictures were taken to Temple Newsam and Reference Library books were stowed in the cellars. The Art Gallery is now occupied by an exhibition showing what happens to books and things of the mind under Nazi rule—the rule that marked its accession to power by burning books in Berlin.

"Books and Freedom," as the exhibition is titled, represents the opposing attitudes of England and Germany to the world of thought and culture. Books banned and burned in Germany, and authors exiled, are contrasted with the country whose eclectic bookshelves conform with her great tradition of tolerance.

There is a film show, with equally poignant contrasts—the work of social services and the churches in Britain, and the work of Nazi troops, tanks and bombers in Poland.

The exhibition is from April 7 to 26—and the film programme will be shown daily at 1.30, 3 and 6 p.m. Admission is free.

ITALY AND MATSUOKA

"Japan Willing to Act With Great Decision"

Rome, Saturday.

Vague hints of developments from the visit to Europe of Matsuoka, Japanese Foreign Minister, are made to-day in the semi-official weekly organ of the Italian Foreign Office, "Relazioni Internazionali."

"The Tripartite Pact," the organ adds, "is more active and operative than ever." After stressing "the willingness of Japan to act with great decision diplomatically and militarily," and "the identity of her interests with those of Italy and Germany," the paper suggests that in Asia Japanese policy is destined to achieve poise in relation to that of the Soviet Union.—Reuter.

The Board of Trade has appointed Mr. Arthur Harold Ward to be Inspector-General in Bankruptcy and Registrar of Deeds of Arrangement in place of Mr. Daniel Williams, retired.

ADOWA TAKEN BY BRITISH FORCES

Strategic Centre in N. Abyssinia

British forces have occupied Adowa, in Northern Abyssinia, it was stated in Cairo this afternoon.

Adowa is an important strategic centre, 6,200 feet above sea level, in a long valley ringed by hills. It is linked by good roads with Asmara (80 miles away), and Adigrat (55 miles). It has a population of 6,000.

STRANGLEHOLD ON ABYSSINIA

This latest success is another stage in the strangling process which Abyssinia is undergoing, and the next important objective in the southward drive is Makalle.

The other main advance to Addis Ababa—along the Addis-Jibuti Railway—has progressed to within a hundred miles of the Ethiopian capital, South African forces being reported near the Awash River.

Sad Italian Memories

Adowa is the scene of two battles in which Italians were concerned.

In 1896, during the first Italo-Abyssinian war, an Italian army of about 20,000 men was overwhelmed with the death of nearly 5,000 white soldiers.

That disaster rankled in Italian hearts for nearly 40 years. Italian schoolchildren of successive generations were taught to "Remember Adowa," and the way in which Rome waited for revenge was shown when the town fell to General de Bono's forces in the second Italy-Abyssinian war, in 1935. Then De Bono erected a monument recording the fact that the Italians killed in the battle of 1896 had been avenged.

Battle of 1896

During the early part of 1896 General Baratieri, who had about 11,000 white soldiers and 52 guns, was hard pressed by the forces of the Emperor Menelik, numbering about 90,000 men, and advanced from Agridat in the hope of forcing the enemy either to retreat or to give open battle.

Menelik occupied a strong position at Abba Garima, near Adowa, and Baratieri attacked on March 1, but in the difficult country one of the Italian general's four brigades advanced too far.

The other brigades went up in support, but each was separately overwhelmed by superior forces. The Italians lost 4,000 white and 3,000 native troops, in addition to those taken prisoner.

LIBYAN STRATEGY

Withdrawal to Position for Battle

In Libya, meanwhile, concentration of British advance forces against the Italo-German thrust from Tripoli is continuing. The whole strategy of Libya is in very safe hands, a military spokesman in Cairo declared last night.

If they push on, we will withdraw until they reach a place where the Commander-in-Chief thinks battle can best be given, the spokesman said.

The enemy already has very long lines of communication, and these are being lengthened now. He also hinted that the Axis will have a lot more troops to contend with in Africa when the fighting in East Africa has ceased.

One major problem facing the Germans and Italians is their liability to feed 20,000 civilians in Benghazi alone. Before the Italians retreated before General Wavell's advance they slaughtered all cattle.

Germans Gain Airfield

With the crushing defeat of the Italian Navy in the battle of Cape Matapan, the Germans are expected to find it increasingly difficult to convoy ships through the Sicilian narrows.

The possession of Benghazi will, however, give the Germans an airfield at Benina, reducing the flying distance from Tripoli to Alexandria and back by about 700 miles.

Italian bombers are apparently being escorted by German fighters during operations, and the Germans are strengthening the air force by putting German pilots into Italian 'planes.

In all its Middle East operations during March the R.A.F. destroyed 178 'planes, losing only 19 itself.

MASSAWA WATCH

R.A.F. Sink More of Duce's Destroyers

Royal Air Force aircraft, says the Air Ministry News Service, which have been ceaslessly watching Italian warships in Massawa in case they attempted to depart when our army approached the town, were rewarded on Thursday for their vigilance.

Five destroyers were observed to have left, and were located in the Red Sea attempting to escape. Bombers immediately carried out a series of attacks in company with aircraft of the Fleet Air Arm.

A R.A.F. bomber dropped a number of bombs near the destroyers. One destroyer exploded and sank when it was attacked, the crew taking to the boats.

R.A.F. Formation's Rescue

Two others were located by our bombers aground south of Jedda, the crews of these also having taken to the boats. More bombs were dropped upon these ships, and both received direct hits, one catching fire.

During the operations one R.A.F. bomber aircraft force landed. A second bomber landed beside it with the intention of rescuing the crew, but was unable to take off again, whereupon the remainder of the formation landed, and returned safely with all crews.

"WEAKENED NILE ARMY"

Germans Say British Troops Have Gone to Balkans

Berlin, Saturday.

The claim that General Wavell's strategic plan in Libya has been nullified by the loss of Agedabia and the evacuation of Benghazi is made by the German Press to-day.

"The British divisions sent to the Balkan and East African fronts weakened the Army of the Nile, which could not resist the Italo-German thrust," says the "Voelkisher Beobachter."

"General Wavell knows very well that Benghazi will not be the last stage in his withdrawal."

The first official announcement by the Germans of their capture of Benghazi was made this morning in a statement by the Official German News Agency, saying:—

Benghazi has been occupied by German and Italian troops continuing the pursuit of the British forces retreating northwards.
—Press Association.

Registered for transmission in the United Kingdom
PRICE THREE-HALFPENCE

Childrens' Wear
Inexpensive but Good
Stephenson's
KING EDWARD St. LEEDS
Tel. 27608

Yorkshire Evening Post

LEEDS SATURDAY, MAY 3, 1941 No. 15,771

LATEST

Good Whisky—
JOHNNIE WALKER
BORN 1820—STILL GOING STRONG

CONTINUED FIGHTING IN IRAK

BATTLE FOR AN AERODROME

Bagdad Claim To Have Repulsed British

Fighting continues at Habbaniyah Aerodrome, near Bagdad, where British and Iraki troops have clashed, it was learned in London to-day.

An official communique issued by the Rashid Ali Government in Bagdad claims that an attempt by British motorised troops to seize the desert aerodrome and post at Rutbah, in Eastern Irak, was repulsed (says a Beirut despatch to the official Italian News Agency).

"The British forces abandoned numerous armoured cars," it is added. The communique also claims that 26 British aeroplanes were destroyed yesterday.

Ankara radio this afternoon quoted Irak radio as stating that hostilities are still continuing, and that the Mosul oil wells and other works are now firmly in the hands of Irak troops.

'PLANES IN ACTION

It was learned in London to-day that at Habbaniyah aerodrome the Irakis surrounded the cantonment and dug themselves in on high ground before opening hostilities.

The cantonment was heavily shelled, and our aircraft retaliated with action against the Iraki, artillery silencing some of the guns. Fighting continues.

It was subsequently learned in London that Basra is quiet, but there is no news as to what is happening in Bagdad. So far as is known in London, however, Habbaniyah is the only place where there are actual operations.

With regard to reports said to have emanated from Ankara that there have been attempts to interfere with the oil supplies, it was pointed out that it can be taken that plans to meet such an eventuality were made by the British authorities long ago.

If such an interference were to take place it would not materially affect the oil resources of the British forces in the Mediterranean, since they are "extensive and adequate."

Iraki Claims

An official communique published by the Iraki Government (according to Swiss radio) states that on the aerodrome of Hobbaniyoh five British 'planes were destroyed on the ground. On Friday 26 British 'planes were altogether destroyed.

The Iraki air force dropped 30 tons of bombs on the Hobbaniyoh aerodrome.

An attempt by British motirised forces to occupy the post of Rutbah and an adjoining aerodrome was repulsed. Several British tanks were left destroyed on the aerodrome.

Quoting a Bagdad repor treceived in Ankara, German wireless claimed that the pipeline from Kirku Irak) to Haifa (Palestine) "through which oil for the British eMditerranean Fleet is transported' had been but by Iraki troops.

Reports that Rashid Ali had asked Berlin for assistance were broadcast by Ankara radio, which quoted what it claimed were authentic sources. Berlin officials, however, disclaimed knowledge of such reports (says British United Press)

IRAK DISHONESTY

Alleged Infringements of Treaty

Rome, Saturday.

The text of a communique issued by the Irak Government, as quoted by the Stefani Agency, is:—

"The Government of Irak did everything possible to prevent the invalidation of the Anglo-Irak treaty, and to avoid an incident with the British Government. Nevertheless the British Government committed acts which were incompatible with the treaty, thereby putting the country's rights and security in danger.

"This attitude obliged the Irak Government to carry out its sacred duty, demanded by the people and rendered necessary by the situation.

"Accordingly they took the necessary measures for the defence of the country's security, while maintaining the self-control necessary to avoid for their part all provocation.

"British provocations against Irak, on the contrary, have been intensified, assuming a decidedly hostile attitude. The British troops stationed at Habbaniyah opened fire on our garrison, who were obliged to undertake military operations, which are continuing with success."—Press Association.

The Truth

Examination of the text of the Anglo-Irak treaty shows that there is no justification for the demand made by Rashid Ali that no British troops

IRAK IN BRIEF

Area (in square miles)	116,600
Population	3,560,000
Army and Air Force	28,000
Police	10,300
Oil production (tons per year)	4,000,000

should be landed at Basra until the contingent previously landed had passed through and out of the country (writes a correspondent). Article 4 states:

> The aid of his Majesty the King of Irak in the event of war or the imminent menace of war will consist in furnishing to His Britannic Majesty on Irak territory all facilities and assistance in his power, including the use of railways, rivers, ports, aerodromes, and means of communication.

Article 5 imposes no condition on our use of Irak territory for the "permanent maintenance and protection in all circumstances of the essential communication of His Britannic Majesty."

"HITLER'S JEHAD"

U.S. Press on Danger of Moslem Outbreak

New York, Saturday.

The "New York Times" has a leading article on Irak under the heading "Hitler's Jehad." A jehad is a religious war against Moslem heretics.

"Into this struggle for high stakes Hitler will stop at nothing—even to opening the floodgates of religious passion, if he can' says the paper.

"This war whose course runs beyond all powers of prediction, has offered more than one strange paradox, but none stranger than this spectacle of the greatest infidel of modern times summoning Islam to holy war with the blood of 14 nations on his hands."

The New York "Herald-Tribune" says, "Greater danger lies in the possibility of the spread of Arab nationalism and Moslem religious excitement to other parts of the Middle East—perhaps even India, where Moslem support has been of prime importance to the British. . . .

"Should a major revolt occur, coinciding with an Axis drive through

either Turkey or Egypt, the difficulties of the British position would be increased enormously."—Associated Press and Press Association.

NAZI PLOTTING

Propaganda Among the Arabs

Istanbul, Saturday.

German agents are behind the trouble in Irak and are reported to have offered Rashid Ali a part in a federation of Arab States. The idea of such a federation has long been the subject of German propaganda.

German sources in Istanbul declared that they expect Arabs to cause serious trouble for England throughout the world, including Transjordania and Palestine, if the British did not soon prove sufficiently strong to control Irak.

They said that these difficulties were expected to coincide with a possible German drive against Turkey and Syria.

Persistent reports are reaching Istanbul that the Arabs intend to renew their anti-Jewish activities in Palestine, and German agents are encouraging such activity.

According to these reports Rashid Ali has been promised control of an Arab federation if he is able to seize control in Irak, although similar promises are also reported to have been made to King Ibn Saud, ruler of Saudi Arabia. The Grand Mufti of Jerusalem, now in exile, is also believed to be one of the German tools.—British United Press.

ARMED BY AXIS

An indication that the Axis Powers have been sending arms to the Arabs in Irak is given in a propaganda statement issued by the official Italian News Agency.

Declaring that Britain is now faced by Arabs, the statement says: "These Arabs are now armed with good rifles and excellent guns."

SYRIAN EXPLOSION

Oil Refinery Badly Damaged: Sabotage Suggestion

An explosion has caused much damage to the petrol refinery that the French mandatory authorities set up some months ago at Tripoli, Syria, says the Jerusalem Correspondent of the Independent French Agency.

The refinery was intended to deal with the raw petroleum stored in reservoirs at the Tripoli end of the pipeline from Kirkuk in Irak, and thus remedy the lack of petrol in Syria.

A great part of the refinery was destroyed before the firemen, aided by soldiers, succeeded in mastering the flames. Some workers were injured.

The explosion has given rise to talk of sabotage.—Press Association.

MESSERSCHMITTS' BAD DAY

Hurricanes of desert squadrons of the R.A.F. again had a successful day on Thursday, when, in a fierce clash south-west of Tobruk three ME 109s were shot down.

One British pilot was reported missing after the engagement.

Within a week pilots of this squadron have destroyed two ME 110s and three ME 109s.

Later in the same day as the fight with Messerschmitts, another patrol from the same squadron successfully machine-gunned two enemy convoys on the track from Gambut to El Adem.—Press Association.

NAZI SHIPPING CLAIMS

Berlin, Saturday.

To-day's German High Command communique claims that in April the German Air Force, surface craft, and submarine units of the navy sank 1,211,000 tons of British merchant shipping and shipping space taken over by the British, of which about 400,000 tons were sunk in Greek waters.

"In addition 250 other vessels were damaged. The loss of some of this shipping also can be presumed. Not included in these figures are enemy ships sunk or damaged by mine action of the nevy and air force."—Press Association.

The Ministry of Food is compiling a register of secondary wholesalers of eggs.

BRITISH HALT ENEMY ON NEW TOBRUK DEFENCE LINE

Both Sides Claim Prisoners in Swaying Battle

FIERCE fighting continues at Tobruk, according to information reaching London this afternoon, which says that a further enemy attack by tanks and infantry was halted by British artillery fire on new lnes of defence.

To-day's German communique, meanwhile, refers to "deep penetration" of "tenaciously-defended" positions and the capture of a number of fortified "nests."

Tobruk, thorn in the side of Axis pressure on the Libya-Egypt border, is giving the Germans so much concern that their oeprations further East, around Sollum, are almost at a standstill.

This is the conclusion drawn by a Press Association special correspondent in the Western Desert, who relates how a patrol from one of the most famous regiments in the British Army penetrated to the outskirts of Sollum without encountering the enemy.

Axis forces which penetrated the outer defences of Tobruk have been thrown back by vigorous counter-attacks, and the number of prisoners in British hands there has risen to 2,000.

The Press Association's correspondent in Cairo says that it is evident that "something has gone wrong" with the enemy's calculations—hence the determined Axis attempt to eliminate Tobruk.—Press Association.

Progress in Abyssinia

In Abyssinia, the Italians who fled from Dessie to Amba Alagi are nearing the end of their resistance, and after making further progress in its advance, our northern column is now increasing its pressure on their covering positions.

The column which took Dessie is meanwhile pressing on towards the chief remaining centre of resistance in the Gondar area, where Bahrdar and Debub have been captured.—British United Press.

BRITISH BOMB BENGHAZI

Rome, Saturday.

To-day's official Italian communique states:

In Cyrenaica there was lively artillery and patrol activity against enemy positions in the fortifications of Tobruk.

On Thursday night enemy 'planes carried out an attack on Benghazi. Some casualties and damage were caused. A British bomber was shot down in flames by our ground defences.

In East Africa our troops in the Amba Alagi sector successfully repelled a heavy enemy attack and inflicted considerable losses on the enemy.—Press Association.

To-day's German communique claims that German detachments of the African corps, during local attacks, deeply penetrated positions tenaciously defended by British at Tobruk and claims the capture of a number of fortified "nests" and several hundred prisoners.—Associated Press.

STOP!

The following broadcast has been made at the request of the Admiralty:—

Masters of enemy ships are warned that His Majesty's ships may make to them the signal W. B. A in the international code of signals. This will mean, "Stop—do not lower boats—do not scuttle—do not use radio—if you disobey I open fire."

AXIS FUNDS IN U.S.

New York, Saturday.

Fear of possible "freezing" of certain foreign funds accounts for the withdrawal of large sums of money from United States banks by Axis agents, according to the "New York Herald-Tribune" to-day

A considerable portion of the 480 million dollars withdrawn during the year went, it is asserted into Italian Government agencies.—Reuter.

ITALY GRABS A PROVINCE

Rome, Saturday.

Rome radio announced to-day that the province of Ljubljana (Slovenia), at present occupied by Italian troops, would be annexed by Italy "under decree."—Associated Press.

According to a dockyard barber, beards are now mostly worn by submarine crews, 99 per cent of other Navy men being clean-shaven.

PROGRESS IN ABYSSINIA

British Capture Town 50 Miles North of Dessie

Nairobi, Saturday.

A military communique issued here to-day stated:—

On the Asmara road our troops occupied Ualdia, 50 miles north of Dessie.

Two hundred native troops in Dessie and a further 600 Europeans and 200 natives have now been taken. The captured material includes 500 serviceable mechanical transport vehicles.

In the southern sector our troops captured a small enemy post at Fike, part of the outlying defence of Sciasciamana.

In the engagement 30 Italians were killed and 135 Italians, 100 natives, five guns and 20 machine-guns captured.

—Associated Press.

BADOGLIO'S SON KILLED

Palo Badoglio, son of Marshal Badoglio, former Chief of General Staff of the Italian armed forces, was killed in action during an air engagement over the North African front on Thursday, the German wireless statec to-day.—Press Association.

"ARE WE CRAZY?"

Mr. Shinwell Criticises Cars at Race Meetings

Mr. E. Shinwell, Labour M.P. for Seaham, addressing miners at Easington, Co. Durham, to-day, said: "I am no kill-joy, but when I hear of 900 cars assembled at a race meeting and 60,000 gathered at a football match I wonder whether we are crazy.

"Merchant seamen are being shot to pieces bringing petrol and other supplies to this country. Think of the petrol consumed, the transport used and the services required, for all this so-called recreation and ask yourselves whether we are really organising our resources for war. This sort of thing must stop."

Mr. Shinwell said that the Government changes were a step in the right direction.

"Before long," he added, "Mr. Churchill will be compelled to listen to the demands for reconstruction of he War Cabinet. There are some members of that body who can be of little assistance. They are occupied with departmental affairs. What we want is a small War Cabinet whose efforts are exclusively devoted to planning the war effort and the strategical aspects of the war."

MEAT AS BEFORE

The Ministry of Food announces that for the week beginning May 5 the meat ration will remain at a shillingsworth for adults and 6d. worth for children under six.

Some of Manchester's 15,000 men available for compulsory fire-watching have started duty.

Above: A foot inspection of the
King's Own Yorkshire Light Infantry,
15th Brigade, 5th Division,
2nd Corps, near Lille in France,
March 1940.

Special!

Light Jacobean 3pc. Suite,
4 chairs and sturdy...... £19.15.0
Jacobean Dining Table...... £19.15.0
Charming Mahogany Inlaid
Drawing Chest...... £24.15.0
3ft. Mahogany Bedroom
Suite, modern design, Tiles,
extra, new condition...

Richardsons
143 T, The Headrow, Leeds 1. 'Phone 21031

Registered for transmission to the
United Kingdom.
PRICE THREE-HALFPENCE

Yorkshire Evening Post

LATEST

GOOD WITH EVERYTHING
H·P SAUCE

LEEDS   TUESDAY, MAY 27, 1941   No. 15,791

Mr. Churchill Gives Big War News

BISMARCK SUNK

OUR LOSSES OFF CRETE

No Conscription In Ulster

The German battleship Bismarck has been sunk.

We have lost two cruisers and four destroyers in Greek waters.

Reinforcements of men and supplies are reaching our forces in Crete, where the issue of the battle hangs in the balance.

It is not proposed to impose conscription in Northern Ireland at the present time.

This summarises the vital war news given to the House of Commons this afternoon by the Prime Minister.

ARK ROYAL'S SUCCESS

Mr. Churchill disclosed that the British battle cruiser Hood was struck at about 23,000 yards by a shell from the Bismarck, which penetrated into the magazines.

Yesterday afternoon Fleet Air Arm torpedo aeroplanes from the Ark Royal made a succession of attacks on the Bismarck. At about midnight we learned that the Bismarck had been struck by two torpedoes, one amidships and the other astern.

She was not only reduced to a very low speed, but made uncontrollable circles in the sea, and in that condition she was attacked by one of our flotillas and hit by two more torpedoes, which brought her virtually to a standstill.

"The Bismarck," added Mr. Churchill, " must be regarded as the most powerful, as she is the newest battleship in the world, and the striking of her from the German navy is a very definite simplification of our task."

Enemy's Heavier Losses

In his statement to the House of Commons, the Prime Minister said:

" The battle in Crete has now lasted for a week. During the whole of this time our troops have been subjected to an intense and continuous scale air attack in which, owing to the geographical conditions, our Air Force has only been able to make a very limited though very gallant counter-attack.

The fighting has been most bitter and severe, and the enemy's losses up to the present have been much heavier than ours.

" We have not, however, been able to prevent further descent of air-borne troops to reinforce the enemy attack, and the weight of this attack has grown from day to day.

" The battle has swayed backwards and forwards with indescribable fury around Canea, and also equally fiercely at Retimo and Heraklion, though on a smaller scale.

British Reinforced

Reinforcements of men and supplies have reached and are reaching General Freyberg's forces, and at this moment of which I am speaking the issue of their magnificent resistance hangs in the balance.

" So far the Royal Navy have prevented any landing of sea-borne invasions, although a few shiploads of troops in Greek caïques may have slipped through.

Very heavy losses have been inflicted on that section of the enemy in their attempts to use the transports... at Great risk, and it is not possible to state with accuracy how thousands of the enemy troops have been drowned. But the losses have been very heavy. (Cheers.)

" The losses suffered by the Navy in defence of Crete have not been... without... very heavy losses of our own.... ... has been compelled ... over... probably without ... considerable... range of ... attention.

Exaggerated Nazi Claims

...exaggerated Nazi claims... ...we have been even more exaggerated than... ...we should not take... ...every aeroplane expedites the...

...we state, however, that we have

lost the cruisers Gloucester and Fiji, and four destroyers—Juno, Greyhound, Kelly and Kashmere—but I am glad to say by far the greater part of their crews have been saved.

" Two battleships and several other cruisers have been damaged, but not seriously, either by hits or near misses.

" Soon they will be in action again, while some are already at sea.

The Mediterranean Fleet is to-day relatively stronger, compared with the Italian navy, than it was before the battle of Cape Matapan.

Our Naval Strength

" There is no question of our naval position in the Eastern Mediterranean having been prejudicially affected. However the decision of the battle may go, the stubborn defence of Crete, one of the important outposts of Egypt, will always rank high in the military and naval annals of the British Empire. (Cheers.)

" In Iraq our position has been largely re-established, and prospects have been greatly improved.

" There have been no further adverse developments in Syria.

" In Abyssinia daily Italian surrenders continue, many thousands of prisoners and masses of equipment being taken.

NO CONSCRIPTION

Reason for Northern Ireland Exemption

Referring to the proposal to introduce conscription to Northern Ireland, Mr. Churchill said the matter had been engaging their attention.

They had made a number of inquiries in various directions, with the result that they had come to the conclusion that at the present time it would be more trouble than it was worth to apply compulsion in Ulster.

Continued on BACK PAGE Column 2.

Launching the Bismarck

The scene at the launching of Bismarck in the spring of 1939.

Skill Beat Bismarck

FOUND BY 'PLANE, THEN HIT WITH TORPEDOES

ANNOUNCING the destruction of the Bismarck in the House of Commons to-day, Mr. Churchill said that while "this drama" (referring to the fighting in Crete) had been enacted in the Eastern Mediterranean, another episode of an arresting character had been in progress in the northern waters of the Atlantic ocean.

On Wednesday of last week, said the Premier, the new German battleship Bismarck, accompanied by the new 8in. gun cruiser Prince Eugen, was discovered by our air reconnaissance at Bergen, and on Thursday it was known that they had left.

Arrangements were made to intercept them should they attempt, as seemed probable, to break out into the Atlantic Ocean with a view to striking at our convoys from the United States.

Visual Contact

During the night of the 23rd-24th our cruisers got into visual contact with them as they were passing through the Denmark Straits, between Iceland and Greenland.

At dawn on Saturday morning the Prince of Wales and the Hood intercepted these two enemy vessels.

" I have no detailed account of the action," said the Premier, " because events have been moving so rapidly since, but the Hood was struck at about 23,000 yards by a shell which penetrated into one of the magazines, and blew up with only very few survivors.

" This splendid vessel, although designed 23 years ago, is a serious loss to the Royal Navy, and even more so are the men and officers who manned her. (Hear, hear.)

" During the whole of Saturday our ships remained in touch with the Bismarck and her consort, and arrangements were made for effective battle at dawn yesterday morning. During the weather deteriorated, visibility decreased, and the Bismarck, by making a sharp turn, shook off the pursuit.

" I don't know what has happened to the Prince Eugen, but measures are being taken in respect of her.

Found by Second 'Plane

" Yesterday, shortly before mid-day, a Catalina aircraft—one of those far-ranging scouting aeroplanes which have been sent to us by the

United States—picked up the Bismarck, and it was seen that she was apparently making for French ports at first or St. Nazaire.

" On this, further rapid-dispositions were made by the Admiralty and the Commander-in-Chief, and, of course, I may say that the moment she was known to be at sea the whole apparatus of our ocean control came into play.

" Very far-reaching combinations began to work, and yesterday afternoon—I have had no time to prepare a detailed account—Fleet Air Arm torpedo-carrying 'planes from the Ark Royal (Laughter because Goebbels has "sunk" her many times.) made a succession of attacks upon the Bismarck, which now appeared to be alone without her consort, and at about midnight we learned that the Bismarck had been struck by two torpedoes, one amidships and the other astern.

Going in Circles

" The second torpedo apparently affected the steering of the ship, for not only was she reduced to a very low speed, but continued making uncontrollable circles in the sea, in which condition she was attacked by one of our flotillas and hit by two more torpedoes (Cheers), which brought her virtually to a standstill. far from here, and far outside the range at which enemy bombers aircraft from the French coast could come upon the scene.

" This morning, at daylight or shortly afterwards, the Bismarck was attacked by the British pursu-

ing battleships, and I don't know what were the results of the bombardment. It appears, however, that the Bismarck was not sunk by the gunfire, and she will now be dispatched by the torpedo.

It is thought that this is now proceeding, and it is thought that there cannot be any lengthy delay in disposing of this vessel. (Cheers.)

" Great as is our loss in the Hood, the Bismarck must be regarded as the most powerful, as she is the newest battleship in the world, and the striking of her from the German Navy is a very definite simplification of the task of maintaining the effective mastery of the Northern Sea, and the maintenance of the Northern blockade.

" I daresay that in a few days it will be possible to give a much more detailed account, but the essentials are before the House, and although there is shade as well as light in this picture, I feel that we have every reason to be satisfied with the outcome of this fierce and memorable naval encounter."

M.P.s' Questions

Mr. Garro Jones asked whether the Prime Minister could say what was the weight of the projectiles which were shown at the Bismarck.

Mr. Churchill replied that he had only heard, about five minutes before he came into the Chamber, the latest developments, and that he had no doubt we should get further information in the course of the day.

Sir Alfred Knox asked if, in view of the losses to battle cruisers at the Battle of Jutland, the Hood was specially equipped with safeguards for her magazines of such.

Mr. Churchill. The Hood was reconstructed to some extent some years ago, and during the war she has been several times in hand for short periods, in order to have her turbine shafts attended to, but no such major reconstruction as suggested of this ship, which was known to be thickly armoured, has possibly during the war, and none had been set on foot before the war.

The Job Finished

Later, Mr. Churchill asked leave to intervene in subsequent business and announced: " I have just received information that the Bismarck sunk."

A storm of cheers greeted Mr. Churchill's words.

Below: Men of the 6th Battalion York & Lancaster resting at Calaleritto during the Italian campaign, 1943.

Registered for transmission in the United Kingdom
PRICE THREE-HALFPENCE

FALLING HAIR

If the condition of your hair gives you cause for worry, why not consult a Specialist and learn what can be done to remedy it?

Mr. H. BRYCE-THOMSON, M.S.P.

CERTIFIED TRICHOLOGIST,
2, BELMONT GROVE, LEEDS
(3 minutes from Town Hall, along Great George Street).
Hours: Daily 10.30 to 7.30, Wednesdays 10.30 to 12.30; Saturdays 10.30 to 4 p.m.
Call or Phone 28246.

Yorkshire Evening Post

LEEDS MONDAY, APRIL 10, 1944 No. 16,681

LATEST EDN.

"BLACK&WHITE"
(Fixed by the Scotch Whisky Association)
25/9 PER BOTT. 13/6 HALF BOTT.
Gt. Britain and N. Ireland only
It's the Scotch

GERMANS ABANDON ODESSA

LAST BIG SOVIET CITY FREED

Red Army Now in Czechoslovakia

Odessa has been evacuated, the German Official News Agency admitted to-day. It was claimed that war material and stores had been removed.

This admission by the Germans came soon after news from Russian sources that the Red Army had entered the outskirts of the great Black Sea port.

Odessa has been in German hands for 2½ years. It is the last big Soviet city (pre-war population over 600,000) to have been held by the enemy.

It is confirmed in Moscow that the Red Army, with the Czechoslovak Brigade, has crossed the Carpathian frontier and entered Czechoslovakia.

'According to Plan' Again

The German News Agency message (quoted by Reuter) said:

In the course of large-scale withdrawal movements on the extreme flank of the southern sector of the Eastern Front, the town of Odessa was evacuated in the night of April 9-10. In the course of the last few weeks, all installations which could have been used by the Soviets had been destroyed according to plan.

The entire war material as well as all stores and supplies were evacuated. The Soviet forces who attempted to hinder these withdrawal movements by attacks with tanks and motorised units as well as cavalry regiments from the direction of Razdelnaya were held in counter-attacks.

With the capture of Odessa the Red Army stands only 80 miles from the mouth of the Danube (Reuter adds).

Largest port on the Black Sea, and the third largest city in the Ukraine, after Kharkov and Kiev, Odessa had a pre-war population of more than 600,000.

It has been two and a half years in German hands. Soviet troops held out there for two months in 1941 before evacuating by sea on October 17. Almost half the Rumanian army was then engaged in the siege.

Drive Towards Ploesti

Meanwhile Koniev's forces are striking towards Ploesti, the centre of the Rumanian oilfield, and Bucharest (says British United Press).

The first main objective is the bottleneck between Galatz where the Sereth joins the Danube and Ramnicu on the railway to Ploesti. All roads leading to this bottleneck are now commanded by the Russians.

Reinforcements of tanks, artillery and infantry are being poured into the Pruth and Sereth Valleys, and swinging southwards into the new drive, which has the river courses on one flank and the Carpathians on the other.

Trapped Germans Panic

The Germans in the Skala pocket are so crowded that they have no room to use their equipment properly, and so panicky and disorganised that they do not know what they are doing. That is the picture of the trapped Nazis given by two Russian war correspondents, Verkhovsky and Galunov, in to-day's "Pravda," quoted by Moscow radio.

They write: "The German generals and officers are all the time issuing completely contradictory orders, and the men do not know what to do.

"Even the German High Command are at a loss what to do, and do not even know what area the surrounded divisions still hold. Transport planes which are sent to supply the beleaguered force drop their cargoes over places not now occupied by the Germans.

"The Russians have forced the Germans off the roads, and the Germans have thus had to abandon all their heavy equipment. For miles around the roadsides are littered with abandoned German tanks and guns.

"The weather is appalling. A snowstorm is raging there at the moment, and this alternates with warm weather, which brings about a thaw with deep mud and slush."

TO LIBERATE CZECHS

Red Army Has Crossed Frontier

News that the Red Army has entered Czechoslovakia is confirmed by General Pickel, head of the Czechoslovak Mission in Moscow, in a statement to a "Pravda" correspondent, broadcast from Moscow to-day (says British United Press).

The Czechoslovak Brigade, under General Sloboda, is included among the forces under Marshal Zhukov which have crossed the border, the General revealed.

"It is now possible," he added, "to launch an offensive movement behind the shield of the Carpathians. What we were striving for long before the war has come to pass. We have become genuine neighbours of the U.S.S.R.

"Nothing and no one will ever come between us. The U.S.S.R. is the first of our Allies to come to liberate the people of Czechoslovakia from the German invaders. This we shall never forget.

"I believe in a bright future for my people, who will rely upon their friendship with the U.S.S.R. Without this friendship we might again find ourselves face to face with German aggression," added General Pickel.

ANOTHER ADMISSION

To-day's German communique (quoted by Reuter) says:

"The defenders of Tarnopol are involved in heavy defensive fighting with the enemy, who has penetrated into the city. Fierce street fighting is in progress.

"The town itself was evacuated after destructions, which had been prepared for weeks, had been carried out."

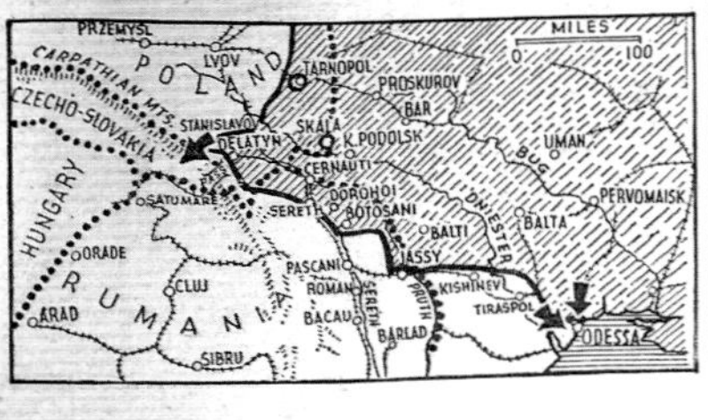

The famous flight of steps leading down to the port of Odessa, which was abandoned by the Germans to-day.

1,400 AMERICAN PLANES SENT OUT TO-DAY

R.A.F. Night Attacks on French Railways

The air onslaught on Hitler's Europe has again developed a day-and-night intensity.

Aircraft repair works in Belgium and aircraft factories in France were among targets hit to-day by strong forces of U.S. Liberators and Flying Fortresses. The Pas de Calais area was also bombed.

The U.S. planes that went out to-day totalled 700 heavy bombers, escorted by 700 fighters.

Last night, only a few hours after the Americans' great flight to bomb targets in Poland and elsewhere, the R.A.F. made heavy attacks on railways at Villeneuve St. Georges, near Paris, and at Lille.

The R.A.F.'s night work also included a Mosquito raid on Mannheim and extensive minelaying. Our losses were 11 machines.

Etousa stated this afternoon:

Germany's aircraft industry was attacked again to-day by strong forces of Liberators and Flying Fortresses of the U.S. 8th Air Force, escorted by equally strong forces of Thunderbolts, Mustangs and Lightnings of the 8th and 9th Air Forces.

Targets included Evere and Vilorde aircraft repair works and Melsbroek aerodrome in the Brussels area, aircraft factories at Bourges, France, and military objectives in the Pas de Calais area and elsewhere.

To-day's attacks were the third in as many days made by U.S. heavy bombers at Luftwaffe factories, installations and aerodromes.

Since daybreak there was a constant procession of strong formations of many types of machines crossing the South-east Coast.

A two-way traffic was kept up over the Folkestone district by outward and inward-bound formations. Two hours after a big force had been heard going out, waves of aircraft were returning from the Pas de Calais region.

A 1,600-mile Journey

During daylight yesterday American heavy bombers based on Britain struck at five German factories assembling Focke Wulfs, or producing components for these planes, at Posen and in the Gdynia area of Poland, Marienburg, in East Prussia, and Turow and Warnemunde, in North-east Germany.

To raid Marienburg means a round trip of 1,600 miles, and Posen nearly as far.

The German News Agency (quoted by Reuter) claims that 50 U.S. bombers were shot down over the Baltic alone during yesterday's attacks. "Very heavy battles took place over Schleswig Holstein and several bays of the Baltic," the agency report stated.

HITS BY CANADIANS

Another Air Ministry communique to-day states:

Yesterday a small force of R.C.A.F. fighter-bombers attacked military objectives in Northern France, and R.C.A.F. Mosquitos attacked enemy aircraft on the ground at Toul and St. Dizier in Northern France. Other aircraft flew offensive sweeps over Northern France and Belgium.

During last night aircraft on intruder operations bombed airfields in Northern France.

Two of our aircraft are missing from these operations.

R.A.F.'s BIG TASKS

Extensive Sea Mining Programme Included

An Air Ministry communique states:

Last night aircraft of Bomber Command made heavy attacks on railway targets at Villeneuve St. Georges, near Paris, and at Lille.

Mosquitos attacked Mannheim and objectives in Western Germany.

A very extensive minelaying programme at great range was successfully carried out.

Eleven of our aircraft are missing.

Paris "Clapham Junction"

Villeneuve St. Georges—about 12 miles south of Paris—has been called the Clapham Junction of Paris. One main line leads off towards the Bay of Biscay. The other runs down by the Swiss frontier and on to the Riviera, the route used by the famous Blue Train in peacetime.

This rail centre has not been mentioned specifically before in Air Ministry communiques, though the R.A.F. have frequently bombed railways in the Paris area in the course of their systematic pounding of German communication systems in France.

Lille, an important railway and manufacturing centre in Northern France, has been bombed many times by British and American aircraft in the past three years. The city's peacetime population was nearly 100,000.

A 1942 Record

A combined British and United States raid on Lille in October, 1942,

Continued on Back Page

Signs of German Attack on Main Front

Little Activity in Italy

Mounting of a German offensive against the British-held Lower Garigliano sector of the main Italian front was hinted at in cables from Allied H.Q. to-day.

Reuter's correspondent reported that small numbers of German troops have been observed on the mountain mass north of Minturno, together with an unusual amount of motor transport throughout the sector.

At the same time, the level of the Garigliano River, across which the Germans may attack, has been forced down five feet by the closing of floodgates on the Liri River, a tributary of the Garigliano, which the Germans control.

British gunners on that sector scored a success after dusk on Saturday when five out of 21 German tanks or self-propelled guns are believed to have been knocked out.

New Zealanders Attack

To-day's communique from Mediterranean Advanced Allied H.Q. says:—

LAND

Casualties were inflicted on the enemy by New Zealand troops, who attacked two strongpoints.

Several enemy tanks were destroyed by artillery in the Tyrrhenian Sea sector of the main front.

Our patrols and artillery were active on all fronts.

AIR

M.A.A.F. fighter-bombers yesterday attacked rail communications in the Rome area, artillery emplacements north of the battle area and shipping off the Dalmatian coast.

During Saturday night light bombers attacked rail targets, gun positions and the harbour of Ancona.

Poor weather over the target caused cancellation of other operations yesterday.

During daylight hours 12 enemy aircraft were reported over the battle area. None of our aircraft is missing.

M.A.A.F. flew approximately 400 sorties.

According to the British United Press, the points attacked by New Zealand troops are at San Angelo and Teodice, three miles south of Cassino, and the attacks were made after the two points had been softened up by our artillery.

German guns and mortars were active in the Cassino area.

New Landings Expected

New Allied landings in Italy are expected soon by the German High Command, according to Guenther Weber, a German war correspondent. Extensive use of smokescreens to cover Allied troop movements in the Nettuno bridgehead was reported by Weber in a message broadcast from Berlin. The Allies he said, are also dropping smoke developers to mark the targets for their guns.

Remote-controlled German tanks have again failed in an attack on Allied positions in the beachhead, reports Reynolds Packard, British United Press correspondent. Four of those "beetles were hit by Allied artillery four miles south-east of Cisterna and three of them completely destroyed.

Seven other enemy tanks were successfully shelled near Cisterna. Hits were scored on a Mark VI two miles to the north, and another was destroyed three miles south-east of Carroceto, on the other side of the beachhead. There has been little other activity there apart from German shelling of Anzio harbour, which caused some damage.

RAIDS ON SOUTHERN FRANCE

Algiers radio, quoting an Allied H.Q. statement, says that Mosquitos, operating from Mediterranean bases, have destroyed three Dornier 217s and shot up several others on the ground at Perpignan, on the French Mediterranean coast near the Spanish frontier.

They also shot up three trains, several oil depots, supply dumps and convoys transporting French workers to forced labour in Germany at Nissan. Freight trains were attacked at Avesnes, Beziers and Narbonne.

Thirteen trains were bombed by Mosquitos in the Rome region, and 23 attacks made by them against road transport.

In Greece, the port of Corfu was again bombed.

Below: A group of the Queen's Own Dragoons in North Africa.

Bottom: Troops cross a jungle stream in Northern Burma behind the Japanese. April 1944.

Crossing a Jungle Stream in Burma

An American pack column, part of Brigadier Merrill's force known as Merrill's Marauders, crossing a jungle stream in Northern Burma at a position behind the Japanese troops.

Registered for transmission in the United Kingdom
PRICE THREE-HALFPENCE

Household Furniture Bargains
5ft. "Jacobean" design Oak Sideboard £38-10-0
2ft. 6in. x 4ft. high Mahogany Display Cabinet £28-0-0
4ft. 6in. Mahogany "Georgian" Wardrobe, wood panel doors, centre fitted trays and drawers £48-15-0
Wing Easy Chair in red velvet...... £13-10-0
5ft. Dark Oak Wardrobe, 3 wood panel doors £45-0-0
2ft. 9in. x 4ft. 8in. high Mahogany Corner Cabinet, glass door................ £24-15-0
RICHARDSONS
143/45, The Headrow, Leeds 1

Yorkshire
Evening Post

LEEDS TUESDAY, MAY 2, 1944 No. 16,700

LATEST
SIFTA SALT
Free Running TABLE SALT
Palmer Mann & Co., Ltd., Sandbach, Cheshire

Franco, in Return for Oil, Cuts Wolfram Exports to Germany

SPAIN BOWS TO ALLIED PRESSURE

HUN AGENTS MUST QUIT TANGIER

Italian Ships to be Released

Franco's Spain, in return for the lifting of America's oil embargo, has agreed to cut drastically her exports to Germany of wolfram (used for tempering steel), and has made other concessions in favour of the United Nations.

Statements to this effect were made in Parliament to-day by Mr. Eden, Foreign Secretary, and by the State Department in Washington. Spain also agrees to:—

Expel designated Axis agents from Tangier, Spain and Spanish North Africa.

Close the German Consulate and other Axis agencies in Tangier.

Release certain Italian commercial ships now interned in Spanish waters.

All Spanish military forces (chiefly the Blue Division) have been withdrawn from the Eastern Front.

Mr. Eden, in his statement in Parliament, said:—

For some time past His Majesty's Government and the United States Government have been in negotiation with the Spanish Government in regard to a number of matters in which the attitude of the Spanish Government in the past seemed to them contrary to the declared policy of Spanish neutrality.

The matters under discussion were:—

The presence and activities of the German Consul-General at Tangier, and of German agents throughout Spanish-controlled and Spanish territory.

The continued presence of certain Spanish units on the Eastern Front.

The detention of Italian ships in Spanish ports.

The level of exports of Spanish wolfram to Germany.

These negotiations have now been brought to a satisfactory conclusion.

Tangier Action

The main features of the agreement reached are as follows:—

I informed the House on September 22 last that the Spanish Government had been asked to put an end to the unneutral activities of the German Consul-General at Tangier.

The Spanish Government have undertaken to close the Consulate-General forthwith, and to arrange for the departure of the Consul-General and all his staff.

They have already expelled from Tangier, the Spanish zone of Morocco and the Gibraltar area, certain German agents, who had been working against British interests, and they are in the process of expelling from the mainland, Tangier and Spanish Morocco, other such agents, to whom their attention has been drawn.

The Spanish Government have given an assurance that the remaining Spanish units have been withdrawn from the Eastern Front, and that all survivors of the Blue Division and Blue Air Squadron have already returned to Spain, with the exception of a few wounded and a small administrative detachment supervising the withdrawal.

The Italian Ships

Six of the Italian merchant ships detained in Spanish ports at the time of the Italian armistice have already been released.

The remainder will now be released, with the exception of the two whose ownership is in dispute, and which will be chartered to the Spanish Government subject to arbitration as to eventual ownership.

The Spanish Government have agreed to a proposal that the disposal of the Italian warships which sought refuge in Spanish ports after the armistice shall be settled by arbitration.

WOLFRAM PERMITS

German Supplies to be Heavily Cut

The following arrangements have also been made in regard to wolfram. Export permits granted to Germany during the current year will be drastically reduced.

Twenty tons may be exported to Germany in each of the months of May and June. Thereafter, for the rest of the year, if as a practical matter they can be made, exports will not exceed 40 tons a month.

It should be added that throughout the whole period of about three months when the details of this agreement were under discussion, the Spanish Government maintained a complete embargo on all wolfram exports to Germany.

The Oil Ban

As a result of the settlement reached with the Spanish Government on all the above points, each item of which marks a substantial gain for the United Nations and represents definite and concrete evidence of the intention of the Spanish Government to maintain neutrality, H.M. Government and the U.S. Government consider themselves justified in accepting once again the strain on Allied resources represented by the export of oil products to Spain.

Permission will accordingly now be given for the renewal of petroleum loadings by Spanish tankers in the Caribbean, and for the lifting from United States ports of minor quantities of packaged petroleum products in accordance with the programme in operation before the suspension of such loadings.

His Majesty's Government regard the outcome of all these negotiations as satisfactory on account of the military and economic benefits accruing therefrom to the United Nations, and because it marks a notable step towards the fulfilment of that strict neutrality which the Spanish Government have declared to be their policy.

WHAT U.S. WANTED

WASHINGTON, Tuesday.

The State Department's version of the agreement with Spain is almost identical with that read in Parliament by Mr. Eden, but there are certain differences, as for example, the following:

One of our objectives was to continue to deprive Germany of Spanish wolfram.

Although an agreement was reached on a basis of less than a total embargo on wolfram shipments, this action has been taken to obtain an immediate settlement on the urgent request of the British Government.

Three Month Advantage

The United States Government, it is learned here, would have preferred to impose a complete stoppage on the export of wolfram to Germany.

Oil shipments to Spain from the United States, which will be resumed under the agreement, total 48,000 tons monthly for Spain and 13,000 tons monthly for Spanish colonies.—Reuter.

Heavy Economic Blow for Germans

By a Diplomatic Correspondent

Drastic curtailment of wolfram supplies to Germany, announced by Mr. Eden in Parliament to-day, has to be considered in the light of other recent heavy economic blows which the enemy has received.

Germany recklessly sacrificed thousands of soldiers in vain to maintain her hold upon the manganese mines of Nikopol, and soon after these were lost to her the Turkish Government stopped all exports of chrome to the Nazis.

These minerals are vital in the manufacture of high-grade steel, and although their loss will not have immediate effect upon the German war machine, the long-term results will be grave and ultimately disastrous.

Germany also receives large quantities of wolfram from Portugal, and negotiations are now in progress in Lisbon regarding these supplies.

Difficult Talks

The negotiations with Spain, conducted by Sir Samuel Hoare, the British Ambassador, and Mr. Carlton Hayes, the American Ambassador, with General Jordana, the Spanish Foreign Minister, have been difficult and prolonged. They began on Feb. 1, and continued until last week-end.

Sir Samuel Hoare, who had hoped to return to Britain for a holiday some weeks ago but remained in Madrid to play an important part in the final settlement, will now shortly visit London.

M.P.s' QUESTIONS

Oil Will Be Only for Spanish Needs

Mr. Strauss (Lab., Lambeth, N.) asked what percentage of the former exports of wolfram to Germany 20 tons represented.

Mr. Eden: Broadly speaking, taking this last year and this year into account, the reductions will be very considerable. I should say the 20 tons would represent perhaps one-fifth or less of the former exports.

Mr. Walter Elliot (Con., Kelvingrove), while expressing the satisfaction of the House with the agreement, said he hoped Mr. Eden would be able to pursue a similar successful policy with other Powers.

Mr. Hughes (Lab., Carmarthen) asked how Mr. Eden would satisfy himself that the minimum quantities of wolfram were not being exceeded, or that the rule as to the quantity would not be circumvented.

Mr. Eden: He can rest assured that that point has been very much in our minds.

Mr. Taylor (Lab., Morpeth) asked for an assurance that the oil which was to be sent to Spain would not go to Germany.

Mr. Eden: We are resuming the same amount of oil products as we previously sent. These amounts are not large. They are only just enough for the bare needs of the Spanish Government, and they will be shipped in Spanish tankers.

WOLFRAM

Wolfram is a compound of tungstate of iron and manganese, and is used for tempering steel.

Status of Tangier

Mr. Nicholson (Con., Farnham) asked whether the future status of Tangier was affected.

Mr. Eden: Only in this sense. The German Consul-General, whose presence in Tangier we have never admitted at all as a legal right whatever, is now removed.

Mr. Nicholson: But is the future status of Tangier in any way affected?

Mr. Eden: Slightly purified. (Laughter.)

Mr Tinker (Lab., Leigh) said Mr. Eden's statement was the best indication we could have that the Allies are winning.

STRAITS WEATHER

Straits To-day.—Dull and cloudy, with fresh westerly wind; sea choppy; much cooler; sunny early sky, becoming overcast later. Barometer still falling.

Building the Nine-Hour House

An "Evening Post" picture of the erection of a factory-made house in Hull in from eight to nine hours. The photograph was taken to-day at the end of the first hour's work. (See "Diary of a Yorkshireman," Page 4.).

MORE WAR FACTORIES AND RAILWAYS SMASHED

An Air Ministry communique says:—

Last night aircraft of Bomber Command, in great strength, attacked a number of objectives in France, Belgium and Germany.

The main objectives were the motor vehicle works at Lyons and aircraft repair works at Tours; an aircraft factory and an explosive works at Toulouse; railway stores and equipment at Chambly, to the north of Paris; and railway yards and facilities at Malines, north-east of Brussels, and at St. Ghislain, near Mons.

There was no cloud, and the targets were clearly identified.

An attack was also made on Ludwigshafen, in the Upper Rhineland. Mines were laid in enemy waters.

Ten of our aircraft are missing.

ACROSS CHANNEL TO-DAY

Liberators, escorted by Thunderbolts and Mustangs, to-day attacked German military installations in Northern France.

German air reports during the night indicated that R.A.F. bomber squadrons approached the German frontier from Belgium and Holland, and then turned away at the last minute towards their real targets.

For the first time the German radio raid warnings were given by a woman announcer from shortly before midnight onwards through the night. Mysterious messages, apparently in code, interrupted the German programmes. "Calling Circular Route 75," said the announcer, speaking very slowly and deliberately. The message was repeated several times over the whole German radio network.

A Normanton Pilot

Flight-Officer E. H. Burgess, of Normanton (Yorks), attacked the railway yards at Malines. "We clearly identified our target," he said, "though there was haze about. We were not caught by any fighters, though we saw an occasional burst of tracer some distance away."

Flight-Lieut. W. J. Murray, a Halifax pilot, from Torquay in the same attack, said that his gunners encountered three German fighters within a few minutes. One escaped, the second was damaged, and the third was destroyed.

"The moon was so bright," said Pilot Officer Robert Sharp, of Kirkcaldy, a Lancaster pilot who attacked the motor vehicle works on the outskirts of Lyons. "It was almost as bright as day in my cockpit. By the time we reached our target smoke was beginning to rise from it. Flares were going down, right among the fires."

Flight Sergeant G. Hingley, of Stourbridge (Worcs), another pilot attacking the same target, said, "There were no searchlights by the target, and light flak was shot at us. The fire was running straight through the target area."

Malines, which has been attacked before in daylight is an important Belgian railway junction on the main line between Antwerp and Brussels, and on the line from Liege which runs through Malines and Ghent to Bruges, Ostend and Zeebrugge.

St. Ghislain, in Belgium, about 10 miles from Mons, was attacked by the 9th U.S.A.A.F and the 2nd Tactical Air Force in April. Their objective was the railway centre.

Tours, temporary capital of France while the battle for Paris, 145 miles away, was being fought, was one of five railway targets in France and Belgium bombed by 900 aircraft in the great R.A.F. raid on the night of April 10 last. Tours marshalling yard has also been the objective for United States heavy bombers.

As Far as Berlin

Toulouse, in Southern France, is as far from British bomber bases as Berlin. The last R.A.F. raid there was on three aircraft factories, which were bombed in moonlight early in April.

Lyons, just outside of which are the big railway works of the P.L.M. system, was visited twice in a week by Bomber Command during March.

Recent attacks in the area of much-bombed Mannheim-Ludwigshafen, in south-west Germany, have been by Mosquitos, the last—a sharp raid—on the night of April 23.

INTERNED IN SWEDEN

An American bomber made a forced landing in Sweden yesterday, says Vichy radio. The crew was interned. Three American planes landed in Denmark, the radio adds.—Exchange.

BATTLES TO COME

Russians and Germans Preparing Way

Although there is comparative quiet on the Southern Front in Russia, there are signs of an early resumption of large-scale battles.

Both sides are attacking communications behind th elines, the Soviets pounding road and rail targets, and the Germans tank and troop concentrations.

North of Jassy, inside Bessarabia, the Germans launched two attacks against Rissian positions, but were beaten back.—Reuter.

Benjamin Schestelowitz [illegible], of Thurnscoe Road, Manningham, and Brian Fletcher (6), of Fletton Terrace, Undercliffe, are in Bradford Children's Hospital suffering from concussion and lacerations caused when they were knocked down by buses.

Below: Troops of the 9th Battalion King's Own Light Infantry (Yorkshire Dragoons) hard at work during the Italian campaign. September 1944.

Registered for transmission in the United Kingdom
PRICE THREE-HALFPENCE

DUSKY MAID STOCKINGS
TRADE DISTRIBUTORS: BARNES LTD., KING ST., LEEDS

Yorkshire Evening Post

LEEDS SATURDAY, MAY 6, 1944 No. 16,704

LATEST E...

GOOD WHISKY
Johnnie Walker
RED LABEL 25/9 PER BOTTLE
13/6 HALF BOTTLE
BLACK LABEL 27/9 PER BOTTLE
Prices as fixed by Scotch Whisky Assoc.

DAM-BURST THREAT TO GERMANS

NEW BIG EXPLOIT BY R.A.F.

Nazi Supply Lines Flooded

Fuller details arriving to-day of the smashing by R.A.F. dive-bombers yesterday of the great Pescara dam, behind the German lines in East Italy, indicate the threat of this exploit to Kesselring's forces.

Enemy supply lines and areas near the front have been flooded, and factories and railways working for the Nazis have been deprived of electricity.

Meanwhile, a wall of water is rushing towards the port of Pescara, pivot of the German front, 20 miles from the dam.

Only 10 miles south of the Pescara valley Allied troops are ready to strike.

Torrents of released waters are flooding the German supply lines and spreading over whole areas to the rear of Kesselring's front lines (says a British United Press cable to-day from Allied Headquarters).

Ten miles to the south of the flooded areas massive 8th Army forces are poised ready to renew the attack on Pescara itself, control point of the cross-country road to Rome.

The mass of water released when our Mustangs split open the great iron sluice gates of the dam swept everything before it as it roared into the Pescara valley.

The destruction of the dam may prove to be one of the master strokes of the campaign in Italy. The wrecking will cause havoc almost immediately behind the German lines and spread confusion among Kesselring's communications. The path of the main flood waters, following the course of the river, runs close to the main Pescaro-Rome highway and one of the main railways linking the German front on the Adriatic with Rome and the western supply bases.

Electricity Supply Cut

With the destruction of the dam vast areas of Eastern Italy have lost their main source of hydro-electric power. The dam was one of Italy's great artificial lakes which supply power to 80 per cent. of the war factories and 12,000 miles of electrified railways. The whole stretch of country in German hands between points north of Avezzano and Pescara itself has lost a main source of power. Hydro-electric works at the dam also supply current to smaller sub-stations in Central Italy.

R.A.F., Australian and South African pilots trained in secret for weeks for this new dam-bursting exploit. They had to pin-point the target perfectly. It was to be precision bombing at its highest—a suicide job.

It was known that only a series of heavy under-water explosions would burst the massive iron sluice gates. At a special air centre picked crews practised precision-bombing and dive-bombing a small target through heavy flak. At last everything was ready—almost one year after the first great R.A.F. dam-bursting exploit, the destruction of the Ruhr dams.

Great Cracks

R.A.F. Mustangs made the first attack. Swooping down in full daylight, they power-dived on to the target, steadied and released the bombs, gained height and circled while the succeeding South African and Australian waves came in. When the last of the Mustangs had flown clear great cracks were appearing in the iron sluice wall. A Scottish pilot made the first hit. Others followed. Bombs rained on to the sluice gates.

Twenty minutes after the first Mustang attack the cracks in the wall opened, developed into a great split, and then the pent-up flood waters heaved forward, and down into the valley.

Debris from the dam was hurled high into the air. Pilots in the circling planes watched as a solid wave of water burst the iron gates.

No Plane Lost

Mustangs, Kittyhawks, and Kittybombers carried out the whole operation without loss. Two direct hits were scored by a South African, Col. Milmot, who said that below the sluices the water was running at high level. "As we watched, the river bed rapidly filled up and the river rose," he added. Another hit was scored by Flight-Lieut. Ken Richards, of Warracul, Victoria.—British United Press.

PLOESTI RAIDS

R.A.F. To-day Makes Its First Attack

R.A.F. bombers struck the first blow at the Ploesti oilfields area in Rumania when early to-day Halifaxes and Wellingtons bombed the railway yards and oil storage tanks at Campina, 19 miles north-west of Ploesti (cables an Exchange correspondent from Naples).

The attack followed raids against industrial and communication targets at Ploesti, Turnu Severin yesterday by M.A.A.F. heavy bombers. Campina is on the main railway line running north from Ploesti to Brasov. Thirteen per cent. of Rumania's oil is refined at Campina.

At least one tank exploded in a mass of flames. Flames leapt to 200 feet and smoke billowed 2,000 feet. When the bombers left Campina was covered with thick black smoke which, after terrific explosions, was followed by orange flame. The bombing was concentrated, with sticks straddling the siding and adjacent production plant and storage area.

Fires started by the M.A.A.F. heavies were visible when the night bombers were 100 miles away.

Bombstrike photographs taken during yesterday's daylight operation, in which 11 enemy aircraft were destroyed and from which 16 heavy bombers and four other Allied aircraft are missing, show many direct hits on tracks and rolling stock in the Ploesti yards and fires among tank cars and freight cars.

At Turnu Severin, the naval workshops and warehouses in the port area were well hit. In the raid on troop concentrations at Podgorica (Jugoslavia) many direct hits were scored in the target area.

OUT TO-DAY

Liberators Attack the Pas de Calais Area

Allied planes were out over the South-east and East Coasts early to-day.

Later it was announced that Liberators of the 8th Air Force, with fighter escort, had attacked military installations in the Pas de Calais area.

SEA MINE MISSION

An Air Ministry communique to-day says that last night aircraft of Bomber Command laid mines in enemy waters. None of our aircraft is missing.

OVER SCOTLAND

During the night there was slight enemy activity over North-east Scotland. No bombs were dropped.

Scouts in Residence

A camp-fire and "cookhouse" at a Scout rally to-day at St. Ives, Bingley.

The rally, organised by the Shipley and Bingley Scout Associations, will extend over the week-end and 18 troops are taking part. Events include a signalling demonstration, bridge building, tent pitching, a camp fire, a night hike, and a conference at which Mr. C. C. Wood, Field Commissioner, will speak. Mr F. Haydn Dimmock, editor of the "Scout," has promised to give an address.

ALLIED "STORM" AT ANY MOMENT, SAY HUNS

Still Guessing, Still Nervous

German anti-invasion troops are manning their battle stations day and night, according to Berlin reports reaching Stockholm to-day, says the British United Press.

A German military spokesman is quoted as saying: "We seriously believe that the invasion in the West will come now, in May. Our troops are ready to meet the storm at any moment."

Some German commentators profess to see a check to the Allies in the slackening of the air offensive (caused by bad weather), but this is only on a par with German guesswork for months past.

A claim that the Allies are behind with their Second Front air offensive was made to-day by Karl Zeppelin, Air Correspondent of the German Overseas News Agency.

"Last week's air war pause was not provided for in Allied calculations," he said. "The Allied air offensive will have to start afresh.

"If the preparation programme cannot be carried out in full the invasion would have to be postponed, but once a certain phase is passed such a postponement is hardly likely."

The answer to this is that Allied bombing is part of a long-term policy. The time factor is against the German ability to repair damage rather than our ability to inflict it.

Rommel's "Tonic"

Field-Marshal Rommel, in a speech to his commanders in his recent tour of the Mediterranean coast defences, quoted by the German News Agency to-day, said:—

"The enemy, whose attack must be reckoned as imminent, will come up against many great surprises. This is particularly true of those enemy formations which will try to land by parachute or from gliders far behind the coastal front. The German soldier knows his fighting orders. Armed with new weapons, he is ready for the utmost."

Rough in Straits

In the Straits to-day, after a wild night, it was cold, cloudy and the sea was still very rough. The south-westerly gale had moderated but strong seas were running. Visibility was fair, with a low ceiling of cloud and misty rain at times. The barometer has risen in the last 12 hours.

FAKED ORDERS

German Trick to Tempt French Patriots

The Germans are issuing faked orders to the French patriots to induce them to rise and strike too soon.

During the last 24 hours warning broadcasts have been going out to France from Algiers. These broadcasts say:

"The Gestapo in France is circulating a leaflet—it is called Order No. 1—from the General Headquarters of the [illegible] movement, North [illegible] De[illegible]. The contents [illegible] tended to make patriots appear in the open before time and reveal the identity of their comrades. Do not act upon this leaflet. It is a lie. It is a Gestapo trap."—British United Press.

INVASION CENSORSHIP

The Anglo-American High Command has arranged for joint censorship of correspondents' messages from all Allied countries in a move to speed up news coverage of the forthcoming invasion, says a Reuter's Washington message.

SECOND FRONT

Three Views To-day on "Impending Events"

Three views to-day on the Second Front:—

Mr. Arthur Henderson, Financial Secretary to the War Office, at Morley:

"The whole world senses the nature and historic significance of impending events. It will be a mighty task."

Captain H. H. Balfour, Under-Secretary for Air, at Broadstairs:—

"Last month's great Allied air bombardment was the preliminary artillery barrage of the Second Front battle.

"Something like three-quarters of the built-up area of Glasgow, Liverpool, Birmingham, Manchester, Edinburgh, Bristol, Sheffield, Leeds, Hull and Bradford, have been destroyed in order that the soldiers shall be helped from the coast to Berlin."

Lieut.-General D. G. Watson, G.O.C.-in-C., Western Command, at Chester:

"The Army is ready and about to embark on a tremendous task—the invasion of the Continent. We are confident."

DOMINION PREMIERS RELAX

To-day the Dominion Prime Ministers are seeking relaxation either in the country or quietly in London, their first break since they reached this country. In five days they have held nine meetings.

It is hoped they may soon find time to visit the troops from their own dominions.

SOLDIER KILLED BY CAR

Sidney Partridge (33), soldier, who was knocked down by a motor-car at Yeadon, died some hours later in [illegible] ...ussion and [illegible]

AND NOW ON TO BERLIN

Red Army Gets Its Instructions

A call to the Red Army to prepare for the coming hard battles was made by Col.-General Tsvetayev in an eve-of-offensive broadcast on Moscow radio, quoted by Reuter.

He told the Red Army that its task was to:

Clear our entire land of the Fascist invaders and restore the State frontier of the Soviet Union along its entire stretch from the Black Sea to the Barents Sea. To do that we will have to finish off the wounded beast in its own lair.

General Tsvetayev gave detailed instructions in which he stressed the need for collaboration between tanks and artillery. "Discipline and skill will lead you to final victory," he added. "Master the art of using your weapons until you have reached perfection. Perfect your skill as fighting men."

Russian Fleet Havoc

German shipping movements in the Black Sea are threatened by the Russian Fleet which has sunk five more German troop transports in joint actions with the Red Air Force.

Attacking by day and night in a running battle, the warships torpedoed one transport of 3,000 tons, sank two smaller vessels and forced three convoys to scatter (says a British United Press correspondent). Then the bombers roared in, sank four more transports and damaged a number of other vessels.

Meanwhile, destroyers of the Black Sea Fleet sank another German troop transport and three barges running the gauntlet between Sebastopol and the Rumanian port of Constanza.

On land, Russian bombers are out attacking concentrations of German troops reported on the second Ukrainian front facing Marshal Koniev's army.

Hungarian Deserters

Hungarians are reported to be deserting to the Red Army, and special German units have been formed to watch over the Hungarians during battles.

Colonel Von Oblerg, the German commentator, said the Russian attacks east of the Sereth are the prelude to a possible new thrust into Central Rumania.

German-controlled Vichy radio says, according to Reuter: "It is believed that the Russians will shortly strike a blow against Lvov and the Polish plain, while the intensification of the fighting in the Kovel sector is interpreted as being the preliminary of another major Russian attack."

Bucharest reports that in the middle Sereth the Red Army is attacking with large forces.

"North-west of Jassy a Soviet night attack with tank support was repelled with heavy enemy losses," Army Headquarters in Bucharest announced to-day, quoted by the British United Press.

"North of Targu Frumos the enemy continued his attacks, which were supported by tanks and his air force. The attacks were carried out in several waves," says the report. "The enemy was repulsed in bitter fighting."

ANGLO-U.S. AIRMEN

"During the day the Anglo-American Air Force bombed with strong forces the Pahova Valley, Turnu Severin and other places. Heavy damage was caused in Ploesti, and there were casualties. Numerous enemy planes were shot down."

POUNDING SEBASTOPOL

The German News Agency reported to-day: "The Russians re-opened their attack on Sebastopol with strong forces after fierce artillery preparation in co-operation with numerous fighter-bombers.

"The German and Rumanian troops," adds the agency, "repulsed the onslaught in stubborn defensive battles and powerful counter-attacks. Heavy losses in men and material were inflicted on the enemy."—Reuter.

OUR FORCES IN PERSIA

Paul Schmitt, Ankara correspondent of the German Overseas News Agency, reported to-day:

"The British Middle East Command has reinforced the British [illegible] Southern Persia by a [illegible] Indian regiments.

"Russian troops conc[illegible] Northern Persia have [illegible] strengthened.

"Other Indian regimen[illegible] sent by sea to Irak."—R[illegible]

Above: The nine Yorkshiremen who survived four days adrift at sea without food or water after their ship 'The Japan Party' was sunk off the Rayonu Maru in Sept 1944.

Left: The King's Own Yorkshire Light Infantry laying a line over a flooded area near Elst in Holland.

Registered for transmission in the
United Kingdom
PRICE THREE-HALFPENCE

LEEDS   MONDAY, JUNE 5, 1944   No. 16,729

Yorkshire Evening Post

LATEST Edn.

FALLING HAIR

If the condition of your hair gives
you cause for worry, why not consult
a Specialist and learn what can be
done to remedy it?

MR. H. BRYCE-THOMSON, M.S.P.
CERTIFIED TRICHOLOGIST.

2, BELMONT GROVE, LEEDS
(5 minutes from Town Hall, along
Great George Street).

Hours: Daily 10.30 to 7.30; Wednesdays
10.30 to 12.30; Saturdays 10.30 to 4
p.m.   Call or Phone 28246.

"BLACK & WHITE"
MAXIMUM PRICES
(Fixed by the Scotch Whisky Association)
25/9 PER BOTT.   13/0 HALF BOTT.
Gt. Britain and N. Ireland only.

It's the Scotch

5th Army Too Busy to Dally for Celebrations in Rome

GERMANS PURSUED ACROSS TIBER

Enemy Transport Chaos

ALLIED PLANES HIT 1,200 LORRIES

Rome is in Allied hands, and the pursuit of Kesselring's retreating forces beyond the city is in progress. A special communique to-day said:—

Troops of the 5th Army occupied Rome last night. Leading elements have passed through the city, and are now across the Tiber in some places.

An earlier communique had reported sporadic fighting between German rearguards and the 5th Army troops who had entered Rome, and had added that our troops then dominated Highways 5, 6 and 7, which converge on the capital.

AIRMEN ATTACK TRAFFIC JAMS

Chaos on the main highways 50 miles north-west of Rome was caused by the Germans' withdrawal. Allied airmen are doing their best to hamper this retreat. At least 600 German vehicles were destroyed and an equal number damaged as they scuttled northwards.

It would be safe to assume, says a military correspondent, that Kesselring has lost over 25 per cent. of his manpower, and nearly 40 per cent. of his equipment in the losing battle he has been fighting since May 11. In the withdrawal from Rome, however, the German commander has probably been able to extricate most of his fit troops.

Pursuit—Germans Watch Corsica

By a Military Correspondent

"The simplest decisions in war" Napoleon warned his marshals, "are the most difficult to make—and the most deceptive."

This is never more true than in hours of great success; it is particularly applicable to the present situation of the Allied Armies in Rome and round it.

The final Allied break-through across the hump of the Alban Hills took the Germans by surprise. It was the capture of the key point of these hills that compelled the Germans to abandon their strong positions in the valleys below.

The Mountain Move

Though they knew that no large attack was possible along the fantastic mountain communications, the presence of a not very large Allied force in the dominating situation of Rocca di Popa sufficed to achieve what might have required costly frontal attacks in great strength.

Now, come back to the simple decision. Nothing seems more simple and obvious than General Alexander's next step. It has been reiterated widely during the last days. He will pursue the enemy and destroy him as planned.

The picture thus projected shows the Germans rushing back along the three 200-mile-long roads north to Foreste, Leghorn and Pisa. Racing in their rear come the Allied armies, with the guns doing another turn of mountain skipping.

This is the kind of simplicity against which Napoleon warned his marshals.

Alexander faces a more complicated problem, and one that has always been the great test for the commanders in the field, as distinct from those operating from remote and centralised headquarters.

New Situation

Alexander is emerging suddenly from the test of battle, with its continuous tactical problems, to survey an entirely new situation that requires new adjustments to the strategical plan. The temptation is as great to the commander, as to the publicists, to urge the simple continuation of the pursuit.

It was because Marlborough refused this simple solution at Schellies, and changed his plans when he had surveyed the situation after his hard-fought victory in battle, that he succeeded in destroying the enemy far more effectively than if he had simply continued to pursue in the manner advocated by some crude German schools.

Let us try for the moment to look at the Italian scene dispassionately. We still do not know how much Kesselring lost in the final stages of the battle south of Rome. The figures

of prisoners taken by the Allies by the week-end do not indicate a collapse, but suggest that many earlier estimates of the total German casualties were on the high side.

The manner of the campaign on the inland fronts rather indicates that the Germans there have had sufficient time to withdraw, leaving rearguards, and placing considerable obstacles in the path of the pursuing force. Finally, Hitler's order suggests that the withdrawal from Rome suggests that the Germans no longer consider it possible to be cut off south of the Rome-Pescara highway.

The position then is that the Germans have something like 15 divisions on the move northwards along the main roads—some may have taken the inland route by the Adriatic route and avoid congestion.

In the whole of Northern Italy there are perhaps five divisions, some of which are fully engaged at the moment in the latest fierce attempt to remove Tito and his obstreperous partisans before the Germans find themselves involved in bigger frays.

Northerly Trek

The 15 German divisions on the move are for the moment extremely vulnerable as a battle force. They cannot easily be deployed for action.

The one thing they probably fear least is a simple pursuit. They have sown mines and demolished roads and bridges behind them. This means sacrificing rearguards, but it gives time, and there are no parallel roads along which Alexander can hope to overtake the retreating Germans.

One feature more than any other that must strike General Alexander about the present situation, where the bulk of the remaining Germans in Italy are either in transit northwards or engaged in partisan warfare, is that not only Rome was open to Allied attack, but virtually the whole of Northern Italy.

There has been no moment when the Germans were less able to defend the Italian coast since the September crisis after the Italian armistice. For 200 miles of coast they have virtually no coastguards. Home Guards, perhaps two or three German divisions and such units as Kesselring can re-form in haste.

Corsica is only 60 miles from this coast. The Germans are paying the closest attention to what may be going on there. They say there are massive military preparations proceeding on the island. They know, more than one way of pursuing an enemy.

A terrific Allied air attack on this open coast is reported to-day. Communications from Cannes to beyond Genoa have been hit. Alexander wants no troop movements from France into this exposed area.

Rome is Almost Intact

Rejoicing People Decorate Tanks

From Reynolds Packard
British United Press War Correspondent

ROME, Monday.

Although the occupation of Rome is almost complete, the main Allied drive is taking our troops through the eastern suburbs. The only Allied soldiers who are likely to see much of Rome at present are there to mop up scattered German troops and to police the city.

Allied troops had crossed the wide plain south of Rome, a distance of 12 miles, in 24 hours, and, tired but happy, marched triumphantly down Highway Six, proud to be the first to enter the city.

Italian women and children ignored the bullets of German snipers to mingle with the columns on the shell-scarred road. They had flowers and wine ready for the soldiers, and greeted them with wild cheers.

Sherman tanks, well to the fore in the advance, entered Rome garlanded with poppies and daisies. General Mark Clark stood on the outskirts, watching the fantastic scene as the first tanks rolled in. Although shells from anti-tank guns were falling close to him as he talked with his field commanders, the General did not wear a steel helmet.

Enemy Rearguards

As the Allies advanced into the city, the chatter of machine-guns became more persistent. The German rearguards were firing desperately to delay the advance long enough the give their main force time to get out.

In the suburbs, the road was lined with German machine-guns, and scores of snipers concealed in towers and trees. They were relentlessly wiped out by the 5th Army troops. The Germans suffered heavy casualties and lost many prisoners as one pocket after another was attacked.

I saw a batch of 60 prisoners taken. They were cut off and confused and did not know which way to turn.

After Two Years

It is two years and 25 days since I was last in Rome. Returning, I find the city unchanged and, except for the wreckage of the railway yards, Rome is almost intact.

On the north-west side of Rome the pot-holed roads are reported to be crammed with German vehicles. They offer a fine target for our planes, and at least 300 were destroyed during sweeps over the escape routes yesterday. The roads are congested for 35 miles, as far as Viterbo.

On the south side of the city another exodus is going on. Italian civilians who fled to Rome as the tide of battle swept over their homes farther south, are leaving to go back to their native towns.

A winding caravan of men and women, carrying tiny bundles on their heads, and leading children by the hand, has started out for, of all places, Cassino.

GEN. CLARK'S SUMMARY

General Mark Clark, commander of the 5th Army, has just met his corps commanders on a balcony in Rome, reports Farnworth Fowles of the C.B.S.

General Clark was quoted as saying "We have smashed parts of the German 10th Army which faced us in the south. We are well across the Tiber. We have almost no contact with the Germans at the moment. We do not know how many Germans are trapped in the coastal area—probably a few hundreds."

COOL IN THE STRAITS

Clouds that brought rain to the Strait of Dover during the night cleared at dawn, and sunshine sent a low temperature up on the 70's by 9 a.m. Out of the sun, however, it was still cool.

A light west-south-westerly wind freshened during the morning and the sea became choppy. During the day the temperature rose a few more degrees, but after a further ten minutes' spell of sunshine clouds began gathering again.

Rome Flash-Back

We are looking back here to just before the war, at a big military parade in Rome, past the Constantine arch, with Mussolini "founder of the Empire," looking on. But now it is "good-bye to all that."

NEW RULE IN ITALY

Victor Emmanuel as King for Entry to Rome

By a Diplomatic Correspondent

King Victor Emmanuel of Italy, will, within the next day or two, enter Rome as King, and almost immediately afterwards will withdraw from all participation in public affairs.

It was on April 12 that he announced his decision to withdraw when the Allies entered Rome and to appoint the Prince of Piedmont as Lieutenant of the Realm.

At the time, it was believed that he did not withdraw at once because he cherished the idea of returning to his capital as King. Though he is retiring, the change does not amount to abdication—he will remain King of Italy.

From Victor to Umberto

Naples radio has announced that a special session of the Italian Government of Ministers under Marshal Badoglio will meet in special session formally resign and that the Prince of Piedmont will act as Lieutenant of the Realm.

It was on April 12 that Marshal Badoglio formed a new Government, which included all six parties of the democratic front. It is probable that when the King retires the Italian Government will formally resign and that Prince of Piedmont will ask Marshal Badoglio to form a new Government. No changes are expected in the composition of the Government.

Rome will remain under Allied military control. The Italian Government's jurisdiction at present covers only the southern portion of Italy, though this may be extended as the Allies advance.

The Position To-day

The German proposals for making Rome an open city were, I learn, received by the British Government late on Saturday night.

The position today remains precisely as stated by General Sir Henry Maitland Wilson, the Supreme Allied Commander in the Mediterranean, when it was declared that it was "the firm intention of the Allied Governments to continue to take every precaution in their power consistent with essential military requirements, to ...

ROOSEVELT TO SPEAK

American Views on Fall of Rome

WASHINGTON, Monday.

President Roosevelt will speak to the world on the fall of Rome in a 15-minute broadcast to-night over four major American radio networks.

New York, Monday.

The capture of Rome has put an end to a black speck in the history of the Eternal City, said a leading morning. It adds:

"It is perhaps symbolic of the wider civilisation that Mussolini never knew that these armies should have been paced by men who fought for Rome without any ulterior ambitions of their own and whom the overjoyed populace therefore receive with wine and flowers as liberators and conquerors."

Impending Catastrophe

The "New York Herald-Tribune" comments:

"The Germans on no line would be much worse off than they already were on the Garigliano. But between the two extremities lies all the difference between a successful stand which might have encouraged the fading German hope and the military catastrophe which foreshadows greater catastrophes impending."

In Washington the news of the fall of Rome was received with restraint. The general sentiments were summed up by Senator Connally, who said the fall of Rome was inevitable. "We are glad that the historic and religious shrines were preserved," he added. "The Germans will no doubt move farther north and we hope to blast them and destroy their armies."—British United Press.

Canada's Pride

Mr. Mackenzie King, Canadian Prime Minister, stated in Ottawa that it would always be a source of pride to Canada that the Canadian forces had a notable part in the campaign leading to the liberation of Rome.

FOR R.C.A.F. IN LEEDS

The Canadian Air Force is to have a club of its own at 67-68, Briggate, Leeds. Premises formerly used as a furniture store have been adapted for use as a club under the auspices of the Y.M.C.A.

Accommodation will provide for about 90 sleeping bunks for men on a day's leave or pass and for 71 expected to be ...

Above: The King's Own on patrol in the village of Elst in March 1945.

Registered for transmission in the United Kingdom
PRICE THREE-HALFPENCE

RICHARDSONS
★ ★ ★
for new and second-hand furniture
143-5, THE HEADROW, LEEDS 1
PHONE 21661

Yorkshire Evening Post
LEEDS TUESDAY, JUNE 6, 1944 No. 16,730
LATEST Edn.

Still the Best! BIRD'S CUSTARD

Mr. Churchill Gives Good News of Landings in Normandy

INVASION OF NORTHERN FRANCE GOES ACCORDING TO PLAN

Massed Airborne Landing

Fire of Shore Guns Largely Quelled

WE USE 4,000 SHIPS, 11,000 AIRCRAFT

Heartening news that the Allied invasion of Northern France, which began this morning, is going according to plan, was given by Mr. Churchill in Parliament to-day.

His main points about the scope and progress of the operation were:—

An immense armada of upwards of 4,000 ships, with several thousand smaller craft, has crossed the Channel.

Massed airborne landings have been successfully effected behind the enemy's lines.

The landings on the beaches are proceeding at various points at the present time. The fire of the shore batteries has been largely quelled.

The Anglo-American Allies are sustained by about 11,000 first line aircraft, which can be drawn upon as may be needed for the purposes of the battle.

There are already hopes that actual tactical surprise has been attained, and we hope to furnish the enemy with a succession of surprises during the course of the fighting.

The battle which is now beginning will grow constantly in scale and intensity for many weeks to come, and I shall not attempt to speculate upon its course, but this I may say—complete unity prevails throughout the Allied armies. (Cheers.)

There is a brotherhood in arms between us and our friends in the United States. There is complete confidence in the Supreme Commander, General Eisenhower, and in his Lieutenants, and also in the Commander of the Expeditionary Force, General Montgomery.

The ardour and spirit of the troops, as I saw them myself embarking in these last few days, was splendid.

Nothing that equipment, science and forethought can do has been neglected, and the whole process of opening this great new front will be pursued with the utmost resolution, both by the commanders and by the United States and British Governments whom they serve.

In the early part of the battle I shall endeavour to keep the House fully informed. It may be that I shall ask their indulgence to press myself upon them before we rise to-night.

So far the commanders who are engaged report that everything is proceeding according to plan. And what a plan! This vast operation is undoubtedly the most complicated and difficult which has ever occurred.

General Montgomery is in charge of the Army group carrying out the assault with British, Canadian and United States forces under his command.

"SLASHING INLAND"

The Allies have established beachheads in Northern France and are slashing inland, according to photo reconnaissance pilots back from the landings, says a Reuter message to-day from the 8th U.S.A.A.F. photo reconnaissance base.

First official news of the invasion was given in "No. 1 Communique" issued by General Eisenhower, Supreme Commander, as follows:—

Under the command of General Eisenhower, Allied naval forces, supported by strong air forces, began landing Allied armies this morning on the northern coast of France.

THE KING TO BROADCAST AT 9 p.m.

The King will broadcast to the nation at 9 p.m.

General de Gaulle, now in London, will broadcast to Metropolitan France.

The Allied landings were made on the Normandy coast between 6 and 8.15 a.m., and airborne troops took part in the operation. The Germans earlier had reported on their radio that airborne troops had been landed at the mouth of the Seine.

The place of the attack had kept the Germans guessing for months, but their heaviest defences had been prepared at the point of the shortest Channel crossings.

Before our troops could land our minesweepers had to sweep the waters off the coast. Other craft had to deal with underwater obstacles, and bombarding ships had to get into position to engage the coast defence guns.

Value of Bombings

It is hoped that the resistance groups in France will give the Germans an uncomfortable time with communications.

The bombing of railways and bridges will make it difficult for the Germans to move reserves. They will have to move the bulk of their troops by road, where the R.A.F. will probably be able to take a heavy toll.

The weather was not very kind to our enormous convoys, and there may have been some seasickness.

The German naval opposition probably will be negligible, though E-boats may be a nuisance.

The naval bombardment went "in the manner planned."

First reports are therefore good.

United States battleships took part in the bombardment.

SUPREME DAY FOR NAVY

Luftwaffe Has Not Yet Appeared

This first day is the supreme day for the Navy (writes a correspondent). They have had to deal with an armada of craft of all types.

"H" hour (time of landing) varied at different places along the invasion area. The timings were adjusted according to the varying natural features of the coast in relation to high water.

Airborne troops were dropped according to schedule.

First reports say that the transport planes returned safely with few losses.

"Going Well"

Gault McGowan, represting the Combined British Press, reporting from an English airfield after watching the second front start from the air, said to-day:

"The situation seems to be going well. The Luftwaffe has not yet put in an appearance in strength, and the masses of manœuvre on both sides are moving into position.

"Before returning I flew for miles inland but saw no German armoured divisions on the move.

"The air umbrella exceeded Dieppe. No outfit seemed without its cover. There was so many of us in the air that we had to get up there by co-ordinated degrees to avoid crossing each others lines."

IN STRAITS

After a shower soon after daybreak there was sunshine in the Straits, although later more banks of heavy clouds swept up from the north-west.

The wind had blown fairly hard during the night, but it lost some of its strength after dawn. A moderate sea was running, visibility was good and improving further.

The sun shone through broken banks of high cloud this afternoon. The sea was smooth, with a light north-westerly breeze,.

Although the French coast was hidden by haze, visibility was good—13 to 15 miles.

A Cloudy Day

Another correspondent writes:—

The Allied troops landed in Europe under a blanket of cloud 5,000 feet thick.

In a flight up and down the French coast we could see nothing except clouds, the flash of flak exploding and a pale pinkish glow in the clouds in the area of the heavy bombardment.

Since the invasion began Allied fighter-bombers have been dive-bombing, glide-bombing and strafing German defences and communications. They are hitting any target that has a bearing on the strength of the German armies at the front.

The fly literally into the mouths of guns and dive within feet of the spans which hold bridges together.

GOEBBELS: Achtung! Achtung! They're coming!

HITLER'S VERSION

A special announcement issued by official quarters in Berlin to-day said:—

"The long expected attack by the British and Americans on the coast of Northern France began last night.

"A few minutes after midnight the enemy landed airborne formations in the area of the Seine Bay, simultaneously making heavy bombing attacks.

"Shortly afterwards numerous enemy landing boats, protected by heavy Allied naval units, approached the coast on other sectors. The German defenders were nowhere taken by surprise. They immediately took up the fight with the greatest energy.

"The parachute troops were partly engaged as they came down, and the enemy ships were taken under effective fire while still on the high seas.

"In Full Swing"

"In spite of constant, violent air battles and heavy bombardment from the enemy ships, the guns of the Atlantic Wall immediately intervened in the fighting. They scored hits on battleships and on landing craft screened from view by smoke.

"The battle against the invasion troops is in full swing."—Reuter.

To-day's German communique says:

Last night the enemy began his long prepared attack on Western Europe, which was expected by us.

Bitter fighting is in progress on the coastal stretches attacked.

INVASION BRIEFS

One of the marshalling areas in England from which the troops were sent to the embarkation points was 300 square miles in extent.

The assembly areas along the British coastline changed to marshalling areas last Sunday, when troops were briefed on their exact missions.

The biggest minesweeping operation in history paved the way for our landing craft and involved 70 miles of sweep wire and 10,000 officers and men.

General Eisenhower spent last night from early evening until dusk paying informal visits to United States paratroop units due to make the landings in France.

About half the smaller types of British landing craft in use are manned and commanded by Royal Marines, and some of the ships carrying the infantry fly the Red Ensign of the British Merchant Navy.

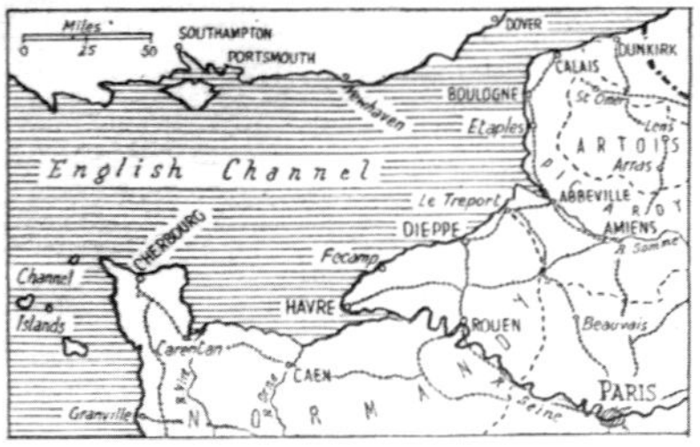

German reports say that Allied paratroops landed 12 miles south-west of Havre at the same time as seaborne troops landed between the estuaries of the rivers Orne and Vire, and that heavy fighting was in progress in the Caen area.

"A BEACHHEAD SECURED"

Tanks Said to be Ashore

Latest reports of the progress of the invasion, received since Mr. Churchill's speech, include the following:

The Allies have secured a beachhead and dug in military circles at Supreme H.Q. heardly early this afternoon.

The German News Agency says Allied troops are fighting 10 miles inland from the coast of Normandy. Parachute troops and gliders have been seen in the region of Trouville (just south of Havre).

Quoting the German High Command's spokesman the agency said:

"Early to-day Allied airborne formations landed on Guernsey and Jersey. They were at once engaged."

The Channel Islands have been occupied by the Germans for four years, since June, 1940. They lie 15 to 30 miles off the Cherbourg peninsula.

The German News Agency also made the following reports:

New landings were made before noon, particularly in the area of Marcouf. Tanks landed in the Arromanches area.

The greatest concentrations of invasion forces detected so far are at Cherbourg and Havre. Obviously both these towns are wanted by the enemy as his principal ports.

A very strong landing from the air was made at Harfleur, and also at a point west of Cherbourg.

"I Saw Them"

An Associated Press war correspondent, representing the combined United States Press, who flew in a Marauder, said to-day:

Allied soldiers have landed in Northern France, and I saw them do it.

From the cockpit of a Marauder which participated in the first bombardment this morning I saw great naval and shore engagements getting under way.

A few miles inland I saw fields strewn with hundreds of parachutes, where Allied airborne forces had dropped. The fields were dotted, too, with aircraft, probably gliders, bearing the distinctive Allied invasion black and white zebra stripe, which was hurriedly slapped on the aircraft late yesterday.

An Aerial View

A U.S. photo reconnaissance base reporter quotes Lieutenant-Colonel C. A. Shoop, who has flown over the scene of the initial thrust, as expressing surprise at the lack of opposition to our air, ground and naval forces.

"There are lots of burning buildings and bomb craters," he said. "[illegible] are burning all over the area."

"We could see our troops advancing across ground at one place. Everything seemed to be moving very fast."

THE "ALERT!"

Communique No. 1 was read by John Snagg of the B.B.C. and immediately afterwards it was relayed in many languages over many [illegible] until it reached every corner of Europe.

As it was being read it was announced that the "Alert" had been sounded in Holland and then in Belgium.

A British voice broke in [illegible] later and it was stated that [illegible] had been sounded to France [illegible] to Denmark.

Above: Officers relax on
Christmas Day 1945 in India.

Registered for transmission in the
United Kingdom
PRICE THREE-HALFPENCE

Clothing Problem?
Every healthy youngster is a problem child? For clothes that will stand a life of rough and tumble, bring your boys to—
NATCO
17-19, Monslet Rd. (Just below Leeds Bridge).

Yorkshire Evening Post

LEEDS   FRIDAY, JUNE 9, 1944   No. 16,733

PERRY'S POWDERS
Keep your Children FINE, FIT & FULL OF FUN
PERRY'S POWDERS LTD., LEEDS

Invasion Forces Make Progress in All Sectors in France

ALLIES BUILD UP THE BEACHHEADS WITHOUT HALT

Normandy Battle Still Fluid

ANOTHER AIRBORNE LANDING

—SAYS BERLIN

Despite all German efforts to prevent further Allied consolidation of the beachheads in Normandy, the assembly of our strength on the shores of Northern France goes on inexorably.

To-day's communique from Allied Supreme H.Q. records progress in all sectors, despite a reinforcement of the German armour.

This presumably refers to fierce counter-attacks by Rommel's panzer divisions.

After the issue of the communique it was learned officially that our build-up is going on "without halt."

The German Overseas Agency said this afternoon that "a third wave of the invasion attack, with new airborne landings in the areas of Carentan, Caen and Bayeux, and with new sea landings in the previous beachheads, has started."

Thus, it appears that the battle which began after the capture of Bayeux is in a fluid state, complicated by the airborne factor.

We seem to be faced by about 10 German divisions in the present fighting. The Germans say the Allies have 15 or 16 divisions ashore.

It is therefore obvious that, while fighting goes on, both sides are massing as much material as they can for big battles in the near future.

A 12,000lb BOMB BULL'S-EYE

Our great air assault continues. Seine bridges have been attacked and Bomber Command last night hit objectives as far inland as Saumur, nearly 150 miles south of the beachheads.

One of our block-busting bombs, a 12,000-pounder, fell there in a deep railway cutting.

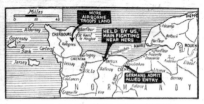

"OUR LANDINGS CONTINUE"

A communique issued to-day from Supreme Allied H.Q at about 11.20 a.m. says:—

Allied troops have continued to make progress in all sectors despite further reinforcements of German armour.

Landings have continued on all beaches, and by-passed strongpoints of enemy resistance are being steadily reduced.

During yesterday there was a desultory firing from some coastal batteries which were quickly silenced by gunfire from Allied warships.

Allied aircraft continued to support naval and land forces yesterday by attacks on a variety of targets.

Late in the day weather over Northern France caused a reduction in the scale of air operations.

Our bombers in strong force attacked railway targets and airfields beyond the battle area. Yesterday morning they were escorting by medium forces of fighters.

These and other fighters strafed ground targets, shooting down 31 enemy aircraft and destroying more

From these operations three bombers and 24 fighters are missing.

Medium bombers attacked a road bridge over the Seine at Vernon and fighter-bombers struck at troop and transport concentrations, gun positions, armoured vehicles and rail- way and road targets behind the battle line.

Fighters patrolled over shipping and the assault area. Twentyone enemy aircraft were destroyed. Eleven of our fighters were lost, but two of the pilots are safe.

Rocket-firing fighters attacked German E-boats in the Channel, leaving one in a sinking condition.

Last night heavy bombers in force attacked railway centres at Rennes, Fougeres, Alencon, Amyens and Pontaubault.

Light bombers struck at railway targets behind the battle area during the night.

Continued on Back Page

TO-DAY'S GERMAN ADMISSIONS

Tank Spearhead Near St. Lo

German propaganda to-day has made a large number of admissions, which, if true, mean Allied progress inland.

The German News Agency reports that the Allies have made new landings on the mouth of the Vire.

This is near Isigny, where, according to previous German reports, the Allies have a secondary bridgehead.

A Berlin military spokesman said: "It is estimated that the Allies have 15 to 16 divisions in two bridgeheads alone, those at the Orne and at Carentan."

Earlier Berlin said it was estimated that the Allies had landed 15 to 16 divisions in France so far.

"Switch Lines"

The German News Agency at noon: "The Allies have dropped numerous airborne units in the areas of Caen, Bayeux and Carentan, and have also disembarked more forces at the existing bridgeheads, under cover of heavy naval gunfire.

"The Germans hurled themselves who against this third great offensive and bitter fighting broke out.

"The Germans maintained their switch lines on the Cherbourg peninsula.

"The enemy tried to reinforce with his paratroops his airborne units and made repeated attempts to cross the mouth of the Orne."

"5-Mile Advance"

German Overseas News Agency at 1.45 p.m.:—

The Allies have driven a wedge from Bayeux south-west towards St. Lo, making an advance of five miles.

The direction indicated in this report, corresponds with main Highway No. 172, which crosses the base of the Cherbourg Peninsula from Bayeux to Coutances.

St. Lo is about midway between those towns, which are about 40 miles apart.

"The Anglo-Americans," added Berlin, "have widened their bridgehead to 62 kilometres (nearly 39 miles)."

"In the area of Caen the situation is unchanged. Powerful British tank formations have been met by German panzers.

"The first battle of material of the invasion, which is raging here, has not yet ended.

"In the Cherbourg peninsula United States troops have advanced two kilometres from St. Mere Eglise towards Valognes."—Reuter.

GERMAN COMMUNIQUE

To-day's German communique quoted by Reuter, says:—

They army has succeeded in strengthening his beachhead on the coast of Normandy, east of the Oran our counter-attack gained further ground.

The enemy tank forces from the beachhead west of the Orne made an enveloping attack against Bayeux and advanced to the west and south-west.

They were stemmed some six miles west of the town.

Our panzer spearheads, which have passed to the counter-attack from the area of Caen, are now engaged in heavy fighting south-east of Bayeux.

The enemy advancing from his St. Mere Eglise bridgehead to the north and south had failed to gain a little ground.

OUR MENACE TO CHERBOURG

Combined Press Correspondents S.H.A.E.F., Friday.

It is obvious that both sides are massing as much material as they can, and that big battles can be expected in the near future.

In spite of the constant air attacks on the enemy's communications it is impossible to stop all movement. The most that can be done is to delay and harass him, and this the Allied air forces seem to be doing very effectively.

It is still far too early to give any general picture of the fighting and of the relative positions of the opposing forces.

The Berlin correspondent of the Swedish newspaper "Aftonbladet" says:—

Yesterday's mass landings have sharpened the danger to Cherbourg.

A Picture from the Beaches

Assault troops landing on the Normandy coast. Background smoke is caused by naval gunfire, supporting the long line of troops moving inland.

YORKSHIREMEN IN THE FIGHTING

Brigadier of the 50th Free After Capture

The 50th (Northumbrian) Division, which, it was disclosed to-day, was in the vanguard of the invasion, includes many men from Yorkshire.

A correspondent representing the Combined Press wires to-day that one of the Division's Brigadiers had an extraordinary 24 hours beginning on Tuesday afternoon.

He was driving in a jeep along a road which one of his battalions had passed an hour or so earlier, when he was ambushed by Germans, who opened fire from hedges.

The brigadier's driver was killed, and he himself was wounded in the arm.

The Germans took him to their H.Q. in a big house, but the same afternoon he escaped, and early last evening surprised his Divisional H.Q., which had given him up as killed, by strolling in with his left arm in a sling.

The Germans did not realise that they had captured a brigadier who was already quite famous, and was a well-known Territorial before the war.

The "Desert Rats"

An official observer who was with some of the troops from the Africa embarked for France writes:—

Many of them wore the Africa Star. Veterans of Dunkirk, "Desert Rats" still tanned by the African sun, shock troops of the Sicilian beaches, soldiers from the Italian battlefront—all gathered, banded together now, for their biggest fight of all.

I spoke to several of them—to Sgt J. Grainger, of Pollard Street, Middlesbrough; and to Pte Ronald Mayes, of Division Road, Hull.

Early on Monday morning a rumour went round that, owing to the weather, invasion might be postponed. The troops now on board ship were on tenterhooks. But the rumour proved false. Ships which had been at anchor began to move, and a rush was made for the rails to watch them go by. Later they sailed themselves.

A Great Record

The 50th Division has fought in the present war in France and Flanders, in North Africa and in Sicily.

During Lord Gort's campaign the Division took a conspicuous part in the severe defensive battles of Arras and along the Ypres-Comines Canal where the German rush was checked and precious time gained for the withdrawal of the B.E.F. to Dunkirk.

From the summer of 1941 onwards the 50th Division fought through each phase of the North African war.

OUR CASUALTIES

The casualties on the beaches of Normandy were appreciably lighter than was expected, says a Reuter correspondent writing from a military mass Hospital in the Hampshire Downs. This view apparently is based on the casualties seen and on a nucleus

---

HAMMERING OF HUN RAIL LINKS

Luftwaffe Puts in an Appearance

Despite bad weather—there was cloud, heavy rain and haze—Bomber Command kept up the offensive last night against railway targets in the battle area (states the Air Ministry News Service).

Marshalling yards, junctions and railway traffic centres at Rennes, Fougeres, Alencon, Mayenne and Pont-au-Bault, lying south or west of the fighting, were all attacked in an effort to block and disorganise the movement of German troops and supplies.

There was increasing enemy resistance to the fighters, fighter-bombers and bombers of the 9th Air Force, which bombed, strafed and patrolled over Normandy until midnight. During the day 10 enemy fighters were destroyed for the loss of five in the first encounters of any consequence with enemy aircraft.

Stiffer Resistance

Fighters of the 2nd Tactical Air Force foiled the Luftwaffe's attempts to bomb the invasion beaches yesterday, when enemy air reaction in the fighting zone was generally stiffer. Continuous fighter cover was again provided over the beaches and fighting area, while Typhoons and Mustangs, carrying bombs and rockets, ranged far inland to strike at German troop movements and road and rail communications.

The Second T.A.F. score at dusk was 20 German aircraft destroyed and others damaged for the loss of 10 of ours. Two pilots at least are safe.

Our bombers were over enemy-occupied territory last night, and to-day German radio warned that single planes were over the Reich.

The Ministry of Home Security communique states that during darkness there was no enemy air activity over Britain.

FRANCE "HIGHLY CHARGED"

ZURICH, Friday.

The atmosphere throughout France is so highly charged that dramatic developments could easily be provoked by a single incident, according to reports from the Swiss-French frontier to the "Gazette de Lausanne."

The paper says that special precautions taken by the Gestapo are immediately broadcast by the ground radio stations which are more numerous than was generally realised.

The population is quiet, collaborationists and the Laval men are in a state of panic.

Some French roads are in condition that only cavalry along them, and then only with utmost difficulty, according "Gazette de Lausanne.—R

STONE BROTHERS
TAILORS TO THE
ARMY, NAVY & R.A.F.
34, ALBION STREET,
LEEDS

The Yorkshire Post
and Leeds Mercury

No. 30,289—ESTAB. 1754   LEEDS, TUESDAY, SEPTEMBER 12, 1944   DAILY—ONE PENNY

DIAMOND RING
SPECIALISTS
Z. BARRACLOUGH
LEEDS 1.

ALLIES NOW FIGHTING FIVE MILES INSIDE GERMANY

American Troops Cross from Luxemburg

BIG BARRAGE ON FRONTIER

Siegfried Line Reached

BRITISH PATROLS IN HOLLAND

Heavy German Losses on Dutch Border

ALLIED SUPREME H.Q. ANNOUNCED AT MIDNIGHT THAT ALLIED TROOPS ARE NOW FIGHTING ON GERMAN SOIL.

They are the troops of General Hodges' American 1st Army, and they crossed the border from Luxemburg and penetrated five miles to a point some miles north of Trier. A fierce artillery bombardment of the frontier preceded their entry, which was made in reasonable strength.

TRIER, 23 miles east of the city of Luxemburg, is in the heart of the Siegfried Line defences, and Allied troops are probably probing the crust of Germany's fortress zone.

British Troops' Best Day

British troops, fighting on the Dutch frontier, have had their most successful 24 hours in the Western Front campaign, killing more Germans and destroying more enemy equipment than during the whole of their advance to Brussels. They captured an important road junction and a vital bridge over the Escaut Canal and pushed half a mile from the frontier.

British patrols were stated last night to have crossed the Dutch frontier in the neighbourhood of De Groote.

HARDEST FIGHTING SINCE THE SEINE

From DOON CAMPBELL, Reuter Correspondent
WITH THE DUTCH FRONTIER.

BATTLE FOR LE HAVRE

Grim Fighting on Outskirts

From CHARLES LYNCH, Reuter Correspondent
OUTSIDE LE HAVRE, Monday.

Strong Defences

Last Ditch at Dunkirk

Converging Drive on Belfort Gap

ALLIED H.Q., MEDITERRANEAN, Sunday Night.

Moscow Statement

MOSCOW, Monday.

Luftwaffe Enters Fray at Heavy Cost

ALLIED SUPREME H.Q., Monday Night.

"Like Wild Dogs"

Supreme German Effort

English tanks heading for Holland, driving past the Town Hall at Louvain.

RUSSIAN TANK ARMY AT CENTRAL EUROPE'S GATE
BERLIN

Forces Menace Hungary from the Transylvanian Alps

A SOVIET tank army, after penetrating the 9,000ft. main ridge of the Transylvanian Alps by one of the highest passes, is now threatening Sibiu, entrance to Central Europe and the great plain stretching from Transylvania across Hungary, according to a statement made by the German News Agency last night.

U.S. WARNING TO AUSTRIA

DAY OF DECISION IS NEAR
—Mr. Hull

WASHINGTON, Monday.
MR. CORDELL HULL, United States Secretary of State, has warned the people of Austria that the time to free themselves and help to restore their own independence is almost here.

M. Massigli

Scorched Earth Order at Aachen
STOCKHOLM, Monday.

Bulgaria Releases Prisoners

Zero Hour

HEAVY LOSSES ON BOTH SIDES IN FIERCE BATTLE BEFORE RIMINI
ALLIED H.Q., ITALY, Monday.

OIL PLANTS BOMBED

Air Support for Patton

MORE than 1,000 heavy bombers of the United States 8th Air Force attacked oil plants at Misburg, Luterbrod, Gera, Lutzkendorf, Brux, Magdeburg and other targets in Central Germany at about noon yesterday, says the headquarters of the U.S. Strategic Air Force.

Big Guns Blasted

R.A.F. Over Ruhr

Germany Warned of Night Raid

PRESIDENT GREETS THE PREMIER AT QUEBEC

"Victory is Everywhere," Says Mr. Churchill

QUEBEC, Monday.
MR. CHURCHILL and President Roosevelt arrived in Quebec to-day. After meeting at the Wolfe Cove Station, where they had five minutes' animated conversation, the two leaders entered separate cars and drove through beflagged streets to the Citadel, where their talks will take place. A crowd was waiting when Mr. and Mrs. Churchill's train—it was named the Bonaventure—arrived from Halifax, Nova Scotia.

The Prime Minister, wearing Trinity House uniform and smoking a cigar, smiled broadly at the crowd, and, giving the V-sign, told them "Victory is everywhere."

France Mentioned

MR. CHURCHILL WAS SEASICK

Stalin's Message

At Work on Agenda

A Military Conference

M. Massigli to be London Envoy

19 Vichy Men Sentenced to Death

14th Army Starts Arakan Drive
KANDY, Monday.

Victory through Light...

A very large proportion of the Research, manufacturing and expert resources of the Mazda Lamp Works are now engaged in harassing the victorious and of the war.

Think of this if you have any difficulty in getting Mazda Lamps for your home.

MAZDA

VICTORY CELEBRATIONS

"Doenitz announces the end" says the bill board sign, and there is a rush from all sides to "read all about it." For some in that crush, this was perhaps the happiest moment since their long toil had begun. All had weathered the seemingly endless bad news and the piling up of set-backs, and some will have known the scoured, emptied-out feeling that follows the news that a loved will never be see again.

An impromptu band fills the street with music, and a conga circles in front of it. The joy, as can be seen in the spontaneous street parties, was real enough: the tables may not have been groaning, but the women managed to rustled something up, and if the fare was not exactly the stuff of dreams, the atmosphere was heady enough. An "Adolf" dummy is lampooned, and a young woman takes a swig of beer from a bottle held out for her by an airman whose days of dicing with death are over.

Above: Revellers let their hair down in Albion Street, Leeds, on VE Day.

Opposite: Newspaper vendors are kept busy as the end of the Second World War is announced.

Left: Victory celebrations in full-swing.

Below: Local residents of Cross Gates, Leeds, celebrating VE day in 1945.

WOMEN WANTED

to take over the

BALLOON BARRAGE

The nightmare of Nazi airmen is Britain's balloon barrage. That's why it is one of the most important jobs in the country to keep those silver fish flying! And the WAAF have proved they can take over this important front-line job from the RAF!

It's a fine, healthy life for women who are fit and strong and fond of the open air. You must be 5' 1" or over, and aged between 17½ and 43. After a short training course, you will be posted to a balloon site. Sites are usually in or near a town. There you will live and work in a small community of about a dozen or so. When fully trained your minimum pay is 3/- a day *and all found*.

In addition to balloon operation, there are many other interesting trades open now in the WAAF. Every woman not doing vital work is asked to volunteer.

A Serviceman's wife does NOT lose her allowance on joining up, and she IS granted her leave to coincide with her husband's leave, subject only to urgent Service considerations.

Go to a Recruiting Centre* or Employment Exchange for fuller information. If you are in work, *they* will find out whether you can be spared from it. If you cannot go at once, send in the coupon.

When this girl joined the WAAF six months ago, to become a balloon operator, she was badly under weight. Now she's back to normal. "You can tell them from me, it's a grand life!" she says.

*Single girls born between January 1st, 1918, and June 30th, 1922, come under the National Service Act and *must* go to the Employment Exchange, *not* a Recruiting Centre.

297 Oxford Street, London, W.1   3010   AR 10

Please send me full information about the trade of Balloon Operator in the WAAF.

Mrs.}
Miss} ————————————————————————
Cross out " Mrs." or " Miss"

Address ————————————————————————

County ——————— Date of birth ———————
In confidence

WAAF

Opposite: A Victory Day party in Ingram Road, Leeds.

Below: Residents of Hillcrest Avenue, Leeds, hold a VJ party.

Above: A street party in Kirkstall, Leeds, on VE Day.

Opposite: Adolf gets his comeuppance as crowds celebrate in Briggate, Leeds.

POST-WAR

The end of the war meant the end of harsh incarceration for thousands of Prisoners of War. They had suffered at the hands of a monstrous enemy which was now utterly crushed. They were home. And they were safe.

Just what that meant is seen in the poignant photograph which captures the moment George Booth, watched by his wife Stella, gives their six-year son Tony a belated birthday present.

The war in Europe ended, people who had learnt the meaning of "blood, sweat and tears" begin to rediscover normality – and the delights of perhaps the first proper holiday for years. While extraordinary survivals brought joyous relief to some, we are reminded that for the bereaved, there is no break from heartbreak.

Opposite: Repatriated Prisoners of War celebrate in May 1945.

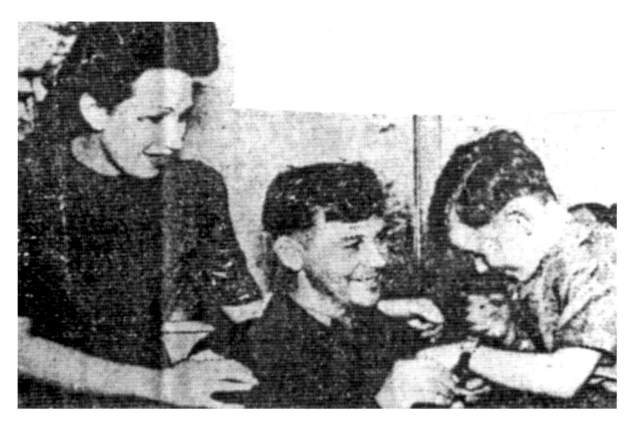

Above: Home in Horsforth in 1945, Stella Booth looks on as her husband George gives a belated birthday present to his six-year-old son Tony, who he last saw as a baby. George Booth's war was brief; within 31 hours of war being declared he made history by becoming the first British prisoner captured by the Germans.

Right: George Booth just before the war.

Far Right: A reunion of PAWS at Yorkshire Evening News' POW rally in June 1945.

Above: Sergent McKie of Hull, one of the liberated POWs, being greeted by Sergeant Booth of the Wakefield 6th Guards Tank Brigade.

Left: Butlin's Holiday Camp, Sept 1946.

Below: Mr P. Weston of Wedderburn Avenue, Harrogate, is photographed in his demob suit, 25 years after it was issued to him.

IMPORTANT

NATIONAL EMERGENCY

IMPORTANT

BE PREPARED

EVERY PERSON—YOUNG OR OLD— SHOULD WEAR OUR

Identity Discs

Full Name and Address—Plainly and Permanently Engraved on Aluminium—Non-Rusting—Can Be Worn Next the Body

Ensure You and Your Family Carry On Their Person Correct Identity Details—*ESPECIALLY THE CHILDREN*

IDENTITY DISCS FOR CHILDREN—WHERE DESIRED THE EVACUATION GROUP NUMBER WILL BE SHOWN

Manufactured to be worn suspended round the neck—easily concealed

PRICE **1/-** EACH DISC

ONLY OBTAINABLE FROM

"Identity Disc," **LEEDS PLACE, TOLLINGTON PARK, LONDON, N.4.**

TO ORDER:—Forward P.O. value 1/- for EACH Disc, made out to "Identity Disc" and crossed /& Co./, also enclose
a stamped (1½d.) addressed envelope and full details.

IMMEDIATE DELIVERY. LAST A LIFETIME.

RATIONING

of Clothing, Cloth, Footwear

from June 1, 1941

Rationing has been introduced, not to deprive you of your real needs, but to make more certain that you get your share of the country's goods—to get fair shares with everybody else.

When the shops re-open you will be able to buy cloth, clothes, footwear and knitting wool only *if you bring your Food Ration Book with you*. The shopkeeper will detach the required number of coupons from the unused margarine page. Each margarine coupon counts as one coupon towards the purchase of clothing or footwear. You will have a total of 66 coupons to last you for a year; so go sparingly. You can buy *where* you like and *when* you like without registering.

NUMBER OF COUPONS NEEDED

Men and Boys	Adult	Child	Women and Girls	Adult	Child
Unlined mackintosh or cape	9	7	Lined mackintoshes, or coats (over 28 in. in length)	14	11
Other mackintoshes, or raincoat, or overcoat	16	11	Jacket, or short coat (under 28 in. in length)	11	8
Coat, or jacket, or blazer or like garment	13	8	Dress, or gown, or frock—woollen	11	8
Waistcoat, or pull-over, or cardigan, or jersey	5	3	Dress, or gown, or frock—other material	7	5
Trousers (other than fustian or corduroy)	8	6	Gym tunic, or girl's skirt with bodice	8	6
Fustian or corduroy trousers	5	5	Blouse, or sports shirt, or cardigan, or jumper	5	3
Shorts	5	3	Skirt, or divided skirt	7	5
Overalls, or dungarees or like garment	6	4	Overalls, or dungarees or like garment	6	4
Dressing-gown or bathing-gown	8	6	Apron, or pinafore	3	2
Night-shirt or pair of pyjamas	8	6	Pyjamas	8	6
Shirt, or combinations—woollen	8	6	Nightdress	6	5
Shirt, or combinations—other material	5	4	Petticoat, or slip, or combination, or cami-knickers	4	3
Pants, or vest, or bathing costume, or child's blouse	4	2	Other undergarments, including corsets	3	2
Pair of socks or stockings	3	1	Pair of stockings	2	1
Collar, or tie, or pair of cuffs	1	1	Pair of socks (ankle length)	1	1
Two handkerchiefs	1	1	Collar, or tie, or pair of cuffs	1	1
Scarf, or pair of gloves or mittens	2	2	Two handkerchiefs	1	1
Pair of slippers or goloshes	4	2	Scarf, or pair of gloves or mittens or muff	2	2
Pair of boots or shoes	7	3	Pair of slippers, boots or shoes	5	3
Pair of leggings, gaiters or spats	3	2			

CLOTH. Coupons needed per yard depend on the width. For example, a yard of woollen cloth 36 inches wide requires 3 coupons.

THESE GOODS M...

¶ Children's clothing of sm... and workmen's bib and brace... mending silk. ¶ Boot and sho... in width. ¶ Elastic. ¶ Lace a... ¶ Hard haberdashery. ¶ Clogs...

Special Notice

Retailers will be allowed ...ther rationed goods up to ... COUPONS. After those da... their customers' coupons. S... limit during these periods th... manufacturer to any one retai... *from your Trade Organisation*.

ISSUED

MINISTRY OF SUPPLY

RUBBER SHORTAGE

GO EASY WITH YOUR TYRES

HOW FAST DRIVING WASTES RUBBER

90% of the world's natural rubber resources are in enemy hands—care in the use of tyres is the most effective way to conserve the nation's available supplies.

Have tyre pressures checked every week. Submit tyres for replacement before the fabric is visible. Never drive a commercial vehicle above its legal speed limit. Avoid driving a car over 40 m.p.h. Never corner at speed. See that wheels are in proper alignment. Never accelerate fiercely. Remember that fierce braking wastes rubber.

Worn-out tyres and tubes are wanted immediately. Take *yours* to a local Garage for despatch to a Government Depot. Or put them out for collection by the Local Authority; or sell them to a Merchant.

Miles Per Hour	RUBBER WASTED
30	NORMAL WEAR
40	WASTAGE INCREASED BY 1/4
50	WASTAGE INCREASED BY OVER 1/3
60	WASTAGE INCREASED BY OVER 1/2
70	WASTAGE INCREASED BY NEARLY 3/4

SALVAGE STEWARDS ARE WANTED. If you can help, apply to your Local Authority; and so do your bit towards increasing the collection, not only of RUBBER, but also of PAPER, METAL, RAGS, BONES, KITCHEN WASTE.

She was a poor-looking thing—

"I set her up on HALL'S WINE"

Think of the satisfaction expressed in those few words! They were actually overheard in a Glasgow restaurant. The truth is Hall's Wine overcomes exhaustion by giving the blood *new life*. First, Hall's Wine is a natural life-force, created by nature's own fusion of more than thirty active elements. Then Hall's Wine is specially medicated to enrich your blood, and to help your blood enrich itself—for your *lasting* strength. Buy a bottle of Hall's Wine today, and you will possess the secret of real recovery this very day.

From Wine Merchants, Grocers and Chemists with Wine Licences. Large bottle 6/6: Smaller size 3/9. Stephen Smith & Co. Ltd., Bow, London, E.3.

(332)

HALL'S WINE The Tonic Builder

CHAPTER EIGHT

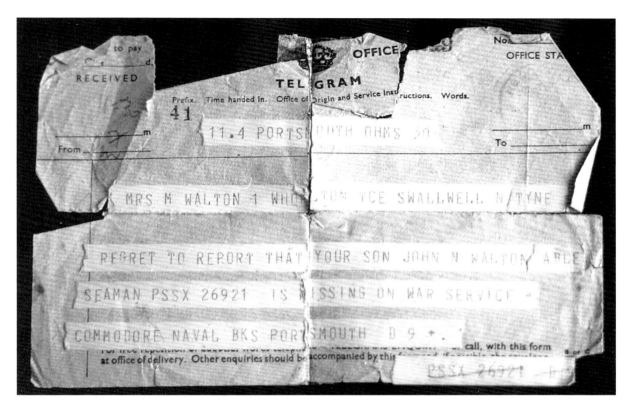

Above: The telegram sent to Mrs Walton in 1941 to inform her that her son was missing.

Left: Norman Walton of Pudsey, pictured here with his wife in 1991, was missing, presumed dead, when HMS Neptune was struck by mines and went down off the coast of Tripoli in December 1941. The cruiser lost all but one of its 766 officers and men. Norman spent nearly six days on a raft without food or water, suffering from exposure and a smashed leg.

CANTEEN SERVICE

The new CANTEEN will be OPEN MONDAY NEXT, SEPT. 29th.

Those wishing to have Dinners on that day should purchase their tickets from the Canteen on Saturday Sept. 27th

The following prices will be Charged in the Canteen

Meat 2 Vegetables, Bread		10d & 11d
Fish " "		10d
Boiled Pudding & Custard		3d
Milk " "		3d
Stewed Fruit "		3d
Cakes		1½d & 2d
Tea	per ½ pint	1d
Coffee or Cocoa	"	1½d

Employees should note that they are expected to provide their own Knife, Fork & Spoon